An Analysis of

Albert Bandura's

Aggression
A Social Learning Analysis

Jacqueline Allan

Published by Macat International Ltd
24:13 Coda Centre, 189 Munster Road, London SW6 6AW.

Distributed exclusively by Routledge
2 Park Square, Milton Park, Abingdon, Oxon OX14 4RN
711 Third Avenue, New York, NY 10017, USA

Routledge is an imprint of the Taylor & Francis Group, an informa business

www.macat.com
info@macat.com

Cataloguing in Publication Data
A catalogue record for this book is available from the British Library.
Library of Congress Cataloguing-in-Publication Data is available upon request.
Cover illustration: Etienne Gilfillan

ISBN 978-1-912303-54-0 (hardback)
ISBN 978-1-912128-51-8 (paperback)
ISBN 978-1-912282-42-5 (e-book)

Notice
The information in this book is designed to orientate readers of the work under analysis,
to elucidate and contextualise its key ideas and themes, and to aid in the development
of critical thinking skills. It is not meant to be used, nor should it be used, as a
substitute for original thinking or in place of original writing or research. References and
notes are provided for informational purposes and their presence does not constitute
endorsement of the information or opinions therein. This book is presented solely for
educational purposes. It is sold on the understanding that the publisher is not engaged
to provide any scholarly advice. The publisher has made every effort to ensure that
this book is accurate and up-to-date, but makes no warranties or representations with
regard to the completeness or reliability of the information it contains. The information
and the opinions provided herein are not guaranteed or warranted to produce particular
results and may not be suitable for students of every ability. The publisher shall not be
liable for any loss, damage or disruption arising from any errors or omissions, or from
the use of this book, including, but not limited to, special, incidental, consequential or
other damages caused, or alleged to have been caused, directly or indirectly, by the
information contained within.

CONTENTS

WAYS IN TO THE TEXT

Who Is Albert Bandura?   10

What Does *Aggression: A Social Learning Analysis* Say?   10

Why Does *Aggression: A Social Learning Analysis* Matter?   12

SECTION 1: INFLUENCES

Module 1: The Author and the Historical Context   16

Module 2: Academic Context   20

Module 3: The Problem   25

Module 4: The Author's Contribution   30

SECTION 2: IDEAS

Module 5: Main Ideas   36

Module 6: Secondary Ideas   42

Module 7: Achievement   46

Module 8: Place in the Author's Work   50

SECTION 3: IMPACT

Module 9: The First Responses   56

Module 10: The Evolving Debate   61

Module 11: Impact and Influence Today   66

Module 12: Where Next?   70

Glossary of Terms   75

People Mentioned in the Text   83

Works Cited   87

THE MACAT LIBRARY

The Macat Library is a series of unique academic explorations of seminal works in the humanities and social sciences – books and papers that have had a significant and widely recognised impact on their disciplines. It has been created to serve as much more than just a summary of what lies between the covers of a great book. It illuminates and explores the influences on, ideas of, and impact of that book. Our goal is to offer a learning resource that encourages critical thinking and fosters a better, deeper understanding of important ideas.

Each publication is divided into three Sections: Influences, Ideas, and Impact. Each Section has four Modules. These explore every important facet of the work, and the responses to it.

This Section-Module structure makes a Macat Library book easy to use, but it has another important feature. Because each Macat book is written to the same format, it is possible (and encouraged!) to cross-reference multiple Macat books along the same lines of inquiry or research. This allows the reader to open up interesting interdisciplinary pathways.

To further aid your reading, lists of glossary terms and people mentioned are included at the end of this book (these are indicated by an asterisk [*] throughout) – as well as a list of works cited.

Macat has worked with the University of Cambridge to identify the elements of critical thinking and understand the ways in which six different skills combine to enable effective thinking.
Three allow us to fully understand a problem; three more give us the tools to solve it. Together, these six skills make up the **PACIER** model of critical thinking. They are:

ANALYSIS – understanding how an argument is built
EVALUATION – exploring the strengths and weaknesses of an argument
INTERPRETATION – understanding issues of meaning

CREATIVE THINKING – coming up with new ideas and fresh connections
PROBLEM-SOLVING – producing strong solutions
REASONING – creating strong arguments

To find out more, visit **WWW.MACAT.COM.**

CRITICAL THINKING AND *AGGRESSION: A SOCIAL LEARNING ANALYSIS*

Primary critical thinking skill: ANALYSIS
Secondary critical thinking skill: EVALUATION

Albert Bandura is the most cited living psychologist, and is regularly named as one of the most influential figures ever to have worked in his field. Much of his reputation stems from the theories and experiments described in his 1973 study *Aggression: A Social Learning Analysis* – a book that is both a classic of psychological study and a masterclass in the analytical skills central to good critical thinking.

Bandura's central contention is that much human learning is fundamentally social. As children imitate the behavior of those around them, and as their behaviors are reinforced by modelling, they entrench cognitive functions that more or less become part of their core personalities.

The experiments that Bandura designed in order to prove his contentions with regard to learned aggressive tendencies show the powers of critical thinking analysis and evaluation at their best. Having set up a play environment for children in which they could be exposed to aggressive behavior (inflicted on a bobo doll), he was able to systematically examine their responses and learned behaviors, working out their functions and understanding the relationships between different aspects of behavior that combined to form a whole. Carefully evaluating at each stage the different extent to which children's own aggressive behavior was affected by and modelled on what they saw. Bandura produced results that revolutionized psychology's whole approach to human learning and behavior.

ABOUT THE AUTHOR OF THE ORIGINAL WORK

Leading social psychologist **Albert Bandura** was born in 1925 in a small town in Alberta, Canada, to Polish and Ukrainian immigrant parents. Despite being brought up in a poor community, he gained a graduate degree in psychology from the University of British Columbia in 1949, followed by a doctorate in clinical psychology at the University of Iowa in 1952. After working briefly at a facility dealing with family mental health issues, Bandura moved to Stanford University in 1953 and has remained there ever since. He served as president of the American Psychological Association in 1974 and received the Outstanding Lifetime Contribution to Psychology award in 2004.

ABOUT THE AUTHOR OF THE ANALYSIS

Jacqueline Allan is a doctoral candidate in Psychology at Birkbeck, University of London and director of the charity Diabetics with Eating Disorders.

ABOUT MACAT

GREAT WORKS FOR CRITICAL THINKING

Macat is focused on making the ideas of the world's great thinkers accessible and comprehensible to everybody, everywhere, in ways that promote the development of enhanced critical thinking skills.

It works with leading academics from the world's top universities to produce new analyses that focus on the ideas and the impact of the most influential works ever written across a wide variety of academic disciplines. Each of the works that sit at the heart of its growing library is an enduring example of great thinking. But by setting them in context – and looking at the influences that shaped their authors, as well as the responses they provoked – Macat encourages readers to look at these classics and game-changers with fresh eyes. Readers learn to think, engage and challenge their ideas, rather than simply accepting them.

'Macat offers an amazing first-of-its-kind tool for interdisciplinary learning and research. Its focus on works that transformed their disciplines and its rigorous approach, drawing on the world's leading experts and educational institutions, opens up a world-class education to anyone.'

Andreas Schleicher
Director for Education and Skills, Organisation for Economic
Co-operation and Development

'Macat is taking on some of the major challenges in university education ... They have drawn together a strong team of active academics who are producing teaching materials that are novel in the breadth of their approach.'

Prof Lord Broers,
former Vice-Chancellor of the University of Cambridge

'The Macat vision is exceptionally exciting. It focuses upon new modes of learning which analyse and explain seminal texts which have profoundly influenced world thinking and so social and economic development. It promotes the kind of critical thinking which is essential for any society and economy.
This is the learning of the future.'

Rt Hon Charles Clarke, former UK Secretary of State for Education

'The Macat analyses provide immediate access to the critical conversation surrounding the books that have shaped their respective discipline, which will make them an invaluable resource to all of those, students and teachers, working in the field.'

Professor William Tronzo, University of California at San Diego

WAYS IN TO THE TEXT

KEY POINTS

- Leading social psychologist* Albert Bandura was born in Alberta, Canada in 1925. Social psychologists investigate the ways in which society shapes the behavior of a population or person from the perspective of the human mind. Bandura served as the president of the American Psychological Association (APA)* in 1974.

- Published in 1973, *Aggression: A Social Learning Analysis* puts forward the idea that people learn how to be aggressive through imitation* (that is, copying), observation* (watching someone else), and modeling* (using someone else's actions as an example of how to form new behaviors). This concept, invented by Bandura, is known as social learning theory.*

- Social learning theory is very important for the discipline of psychology (the study of human thought and behavior). The theory's arrival marked a turning point in psychological research as it bridged the gap between behaviorism* (a school of thought arguing that human action can be viewed as a process of responses to any given stimulus), cognition* (the working processes of the brain that enable us to learn about and understand our environment), and social psychology.*

Who Is Albert Bandura?

Albert Bandura, the author of *Aggression: A Social Learning Analysis* (1973), was born in Alberta, Canada in 1925. His mother was Polish and his father was Ukrainian, and they had both independently immigrated to Canada earlier in their lives. Despite not having much money, Bandura's parents managed to buy some land to run a small farm. They believed in the power of education. As Albert Bandura states, "My parents had no schooling, but they placed a high value on the education they missed. My father taught himself to read three languages and served as a member of the school board in the district where we lived."

Encouraged by his parents to get a higher education, Bandura attended the University of British Columbia and gained his graduate degree in psychology there in 1949. He continued his studies as a postgraduate at the University of Iowa, where he obtained his master's degree and doctorate in clinical psychology by 1952. It was also at this time that he married his wife, Virginia. After a brief internship at the Wichita Guidance Center—a facility supporting adults and children with family mental health problems—Bandura joined Stanford University in 1953, where he has remained ever since.

Bandura has received many accolades throughout his career and is currently the David Starr Jordan Professor Emeritus of Social Science at Stanford. He was elected to the National Academy of Sciences, served as president of the American Psychological Association (the APA) in 1974, received the APA's Award for Distinguished Scientific Contributions in 1980 and its Outstanding Lifetime Contribution to Psychology in 2004. Colleges and universities around the world have awarded him numerous honorary degrees.

What Does *Aggression: A Social Learning Analysis* Say?

Aggression claims that aggression is a behavior that a person learns and that it develops early in life. Bandura argues that aggressive behavior is learned through three main processes:

- Imitation
- Observation
- Modeling

Bandura grouped his study of those processes collectively into what he called social learning theory.

By "imitation," Bandura means learning by copying someone else's behavior. When a child learns to speak, for example, the mother often encourages copying by leaning close to the child so he or she can see how the mother's mouth shapes a word. By "observation," he means learning by watching another's behavior (as occurs when a child who sees his or her parent treat an animal badly may then do the same). By "modeling," he means using the actions of another as an example of how to form new behaviors. If a parent always reacts angrily to new situations, for example, then the child will react to new situations in a similar manner.

Previous theories argued that behavior represented a simple, automatic response to environmental cues. For Bandura, however, humans are cerebral (that is, thinking), self-regulating beings who have a degree of influence on their environment. Later termed social cognitive theory,* this viewpoint, alongside much of Bandura's other work, helped create a major shift towards what is called cognitive psychology:* the school of psychology concerned with how cognition (the process of gaining knowledge involving thinking, problem solving, learning, and the like) influences behavior. It moved psychology in a different direction and away from the psychoanalytic* and evolutionary theories of the past.

Psychoanalysis, a school of thought that the famous Austrian psychologist Sigmund Freud* founded, tries to explain human behavior by understanding unconscious drives and problems in early development. In *Aggression*, Bandura also relies heavily on measurable data to test his thoughts and beliefs—something that was relatively new in social psychology at the time.

Bandura's work is among the most cited scholarship since the birth of psychology as a discipline. In an article published in the *Review of General Psychology*, Bandura is ranked the fourth most eminent psychologist of the twentieth century, and he is the fifth most cited psychologist in psychology journals. He has been credited with improving virtually all specialist areas within the field, from cognitive to experimental to counseling psychology* (the use of both theory and practice to help patients through emotional problems).

Bandura was publishing on aggression as early as 1960 and later focused on adolescents and children. Much of what we now know about the impact of the early childhood environment on delinquency (criminal acts performed by young people) and anti-social behavior can be traced back to Bandura's work. To this day, his theories influence government policy, healthcare, education, legal work, early years' care, and social-service practice.

The dedication from the American Psychological Association on the presentation of Bandura's award in 2004 stated: "The American Psychological Association is honored to recognize your outstanding contributions to psychology as one of the most eminent psychologists of the twentieth century, as psychology's most cited contributor for your many influential theories, innovative experimental research programs, and significant applications of that wisdom to practical domains. Reflected in your research publications is an admirable grasp of fundamental theoretical issues, analytic and methodological rigor, and highly fruitful approaches to complex psychosocial problems. Your brilliant scholarship has been an invaluable resource for academics, practitioners, and public policymakers."

Why Does *Aggression* Matter?

Aggression is essential reading for anyone interested in social psychology. It formed the basis of Bandura's version of social learning theory, and it is often cited as the foundation of social psychology. The theories proposed in *Aggression* offer the reader a different view on why humans behave the way they do. They particularly focus on how we learn by means of modeling, imitation, and observation.

Bandura is also an important figure in the field of experimental psychology. Measuring behavior quantitatively*—using concrete data, like reaction times or height—was relatively new at the time. Previously, psychologists mainly put their faith in subjective measures and individual case studies. They studied behavior by observing one person rather than by making assertions using statistically significant numbers of participants. This in turn meant that generalizing findings in psychology was difficult.

Bandura described many ways of doing things that have become significant, such as the Bobo doll experiments,* in which children would become more violent when they were exposed to adults being violent. Those experiments have particular relevance today, when arguments against violent music videos, movies, and computer games focus on the negative impacts that such things have on children and young people.

Understanding Bandura's work opens avenues into other ideas and theories, too. The American psychologist B. F. Skinner's* behaviorist* theories, according to which human action is a response to a given stimulus, has significantly influenced social learning theories. Bandura used behaviorism as a starting point, and much of his work builds on it. He suggested, however, that ideas about "stimulus-response"—according to which behavior is a direct effect of incoming signals (aggression, for example, is a direct result of frustration)—underestimated the complexity of cognition. Understanding this can help us to resist simplistic and theoretical models of behavior.

At the time Bandura was writing *Aggression* in 1973, the world was in the grip of radical social change. Three major historic events all contributed to a feeling of heightened tension among some Americans: the Civil Rights Movement* that demanded equality for minority groups, the Vietnam War* that saw the United States bogged down in a war against Vietnamese communism,* and the Cold War* that pitted the United States against the Soviet Union* in an ideological and military standoff. Despite those wrenching events, *Aggression* is an optimistic piece of work. It says that if we can *understand* aggressive behavior, we can *treat* it.

Given that violence continues to be a part of modern society, Bandura's arguments are as significant now as they were when he first proposed them.

SECTION 1
INFLUENCES

MODULE 1
THE AUTHOR AND THE HISTORICAL CONTEXT

KEY POINTS

- *Aggression* is one of the most quoted psychological works of all time.

- Albert Bandura's humble beginnings influenced his attitude towards the learning environment that he explored in *Aggression.*

- America was going through a period of immense unrest as Bandura was writing *Aggression*. World War II,* the Vietnam War,* and the escalating threat of the use of nuclear weapons may have fueled the need to understand aggressive behavior.

Why Read This Text?

Albert Bandura's *Aggression: A Social Learning Analysis* (1973) is the seminal work of an academic whom the International Union of Psychological Science calls "one of the most influential psychologists ever, and the most frequently cited living psychologist." Bandura was president of the American Psychological Association (APA) in 1974, has been ranked as the fourth most eminent psychologist of the twentieth century, and he is the fifth most cited scholar in psychology journals. At 89 years old, he is still a professor at Stanford University, where he has worked for the last 62 years.

Aggression marks a shift in explanations of social action, combining cognition* (the working processes of the brain that enable us to learn about and understand our environment) with behaviorism* (the understanding that human action can be considered as a process of

> 66 With the progressive growth of instruments of destruction … the hazards of ill-judged actions have thus become enormously magnified. Man's aggressive potential has also been increased. 99
>
> Albert Bandura, *Aggression: A Social Learning Analysis*

responses to any given stimulus). Bandura joins these theoretical viewpoints into a new social learning theory* to provide an entirely new framework within which to view social behavior.

Social learning theory argues that learning occurs by means of the social processes of observation, imitation, and modeling. Although this particular book focuses on aggression, it can be used to describe a great deal of human activity. Bandura also shares in it much empirical* data (data verifiable by observation) to support his hypotheses, which, while standard in other sciences, was at the time an emerging methodology in psychology.

Bandura's work, then, not only marked a departure from psychoanalytic* and evolutionary* explanations of behavior (that is, explanation that looked at unconscious causes of human behavior or causes with their roots in the deep history of our species) but also helped to solidify psychology as a quantitative scientific endeavor. It is hard to imagine what psychology would look like today had it not been for Bandura's work.

Author's Life

Albert Bandura's parents emphasized the importance of education. He spent his childhood in a small Canadian town that offered little in terms of educational resources. His school had only two teachers, few textbooks, and limited equipment. That helped to motivate Bandura to develop a self-directed approach to his own learning. He said of his early life, "The paucity of educational resources turned out to be an enabling factor which has served me well rather than an insurmountable handicapping one. The content of courses is perishable, but self-regulatory skills have lasting functional value whatever the pursuit might be … The road I have traveled is very much in keeping with the agentic* perspective toward human self-development, adaptation, and change, which underpins social cognitive theory."[1]

By "agentic," he means the idea that people both produce social conditions and are affected by them. His parents' focus on the importance of hard work clearly played an important role in forming his outlook and influenced his ideas about social cognition. He quotes his mother as saying, "You have a choice. You can work in the field and get drunk in the beer parlor, or you might get an education."[2]

Author's Background

Bandura started to write *Aggression* around 1970, while at Stanford University. He comments in the preface that the project began when he was in residence as a fellow at the Center for Advanced Study in the Behavioral Sciences, which had suffered a violent attack that year. This is presumably a reference to an arson attack that destroyed decades of work "by a prominent scholar from India."[3] At the time that Bandura was writing *Aggression*, the Stanford campus was a highly politically charged place. The unexplained violent incident directed against an academic like himself obviously caught his attention.

Frequent protests were occurring on the campus. Opposition to the Vietnam War* and nuclear arms race* and support for the Civil Rights Movement* (the movement for equal social and political rights for black Americans) still reverberated.[4] It could be argued that Bandura's studies on aggression were linked to this flux within American and world history. The pace of technological development, the threat of nuclear weapons, and the mass ownership of television were also posing interesting psychological questions. These issues were of particular relevance to Bandura's views regarding social learning and aggression.

NOTES

1   Albert Bandura, "Autobiography," in *A History of Psychology in Autobiography*, vol. 9, eds. M. G. Lindzey and W. M. Runyan (Washington, DC: American Psychological Association, 2007), 42–74.

2   Christine Foster, "Confidence Man," *Stanford Magazine*, September/ October 2006, http://alumni.stanford.edu/get/page/magazine/ article/?article_id=33332.

3   Susan Wels, "The Troubles at Stanford: Student Uprisings in the 1960s and '70s," *Sandstone and Tile* 35, no. 1 (2011).

4   Wels, "The Troubles at Stanford."

MODULE 2
ACADEMIC CONTEXT

KEY POINTS

- At the time of writing *Aggression*, attempts by psychologists to explain human behavior mostly concerned the emergent theories of behaviorist B. F. Skinner* and psychoanalytic* theories—those offering explanations of the unconscious process that drove human behavior, first proposed by the founder of the therapeutic and theoretical field of psychoanalysis, Sigmund Freud.*

- *Aggression* ushered in a new era in social psychology (psychological inquiry with a focus on the role of society) in which researchers and academics became aware of the role that mental processes ("cognition")* play in social learning and behavior.

- Social learning theory describes the idea that people learn not only by directly performing a task but also by means of three main social processes: observation,* modeling,* and imitation.*

The Work in its Context

Despite its importance now to the field of social psychology, it is difficult to place Bandura's *Aggression: A Social Learning Analysis* solidly in any particular school of thought. He helped to bring about a paradigm shift in psychology—a fundamental change in the intellectual framework by which phenomena are explained and understood—by explaining human action using both cognitive psychology* and behaviorism,* while arguing that the role of psychoanalytic theory* had been overstated. Behaviorism* is the school of thought that human action can be viewed as a process of

> ❝ Man's technological capacity for massive destruction has now developed to the point where he can no longer continue to settle conflicts by destructive means. ❞
>
> Albert Bandura, *Aggression: A Social Learning Analysis*

responses to stimuli. Psychoanalytic explanations of behavior commonly focus on the role of unconscious mental operations. Cognitive psychology* is concerned with the way in which the mind processes information.

Bandura initially shared the behaviorist view that B. F. Skinner perpetuated. But he extended Skinner's theories significantly, believing that his models of behavior were far too simple. Behaviorists used controlled experiments on animals—that is, experiments with a "control group" of animals that were not interfered with in the same way as the other animals in the experiment—to collect evidence to test their hypotheses that external environmental factors caused human behavior. In *Aggression*, Bandura continues and builds upon behaviorists' reliance on empirical* data (data verifiable by observation).

Arguably, *Social Learning and Imitation*,[1] by American psychologists John Dollard* and Neal Miller,* influenced Bandura's concept of social learning theory. Like the behaviorists, Dollard and Miller used animal experiments to generate much of their theory and saw imitation as a mostly independent, rather than social, process. Bandura recognized the incomplete nature of their study but used its basic principles to explore aggression in adolescent boys.[2] This unique approach of looking at aggression from the perspective of social learning and social processes aided him in developing his theories.

As Bandura has described, Stanford University gave him the freedom to pursue his research goals: "I was blessed with illustrious colleagues, gifted students, considerable freedom to go wherever my curiosity might lead, and a university ethos that approached scholarship not as a matter of publish or perish, but with puzzlement that the pursuit of knowledge should require coercion."[3]

Even in his early years at the universities of Vancouver and Iowa, where Bandura was a junior researcher, he was given opportunities to earn money and provided with financial aid. Throughout his career, he benefited from a rare level of academic freedom.

Overview of the Field

The idea of social learning was relatively new and underdeveloped prior to Bandura's work; certainly, the concept had not been significantly applied to aggression. Bandura drew inspiration from Skinner's ideas on operant conditioning,* according to which behavior is learned by means of reinforcement or punishment.

For example: if you give a rat some food as a reward for performing an action, the rat is likely to repeat it; conversely, if you give a rat an electric shock when it performs an action, it is more likely to avoid the action in future. Bandura extended those theories from rats to human development in order to explain that aggressive acts can result from learning through social processes rather than just from direct experience.

At the time of writing *Aggression*, Bandura was in the process of breaking away from received wisdom regarding aggression and learning. At that point, two main theories of why people behave aggressively were most influential: the instinctual theory* and the drive theory.*

The instinctual theory suggests that aggression is an evolutionary trait or instinct: it is an essential aspect of being human as it helps humanity survive and reproduce. This theory is Darwinian* in nature (that is, it follows principles first articulated by the naturalist Charles Darwin* concerning the processes that drive evolution). It maintains that aggressive behavior can be explained by considering the deep history of our species: "Aggressive behaviors in animals, for example, threat, attack, and defense, are commonly related to competition over resources, competition over mating opportunities, or fights for survival."[4]

The drive theory suggests that we are all born with specific psychological impulses, such as the need for comfort, and that all behavior is geared towards satisfying these innate impulses. This theory contends that when something interrupts our efforts to satisfy these impulses, negative behaviors, such as aggression, result. These theories were originally inspired by psychoanalytic ideas. The predominantly accepted aspect of drive theory was that aggression was a result of frustration:[5] the "frustration–aggression hypothesis."

Academic Influences

Bandura was influenced by the early psychoanalysts—as were most scholars interested in behavioral development—and also the work of the behaviorists, who had shown that behavior can be taught to animals using a system of reward and punishment. For example, the radical behaviorist B. F. Skinner had shown that pigeons could be trained using such a program to perform complex actions like playing table tennis.[6]

Another influence was Bandura's colleague Robert Sears, a major proponent of social learning. Although they often disagreed theoretically, it has been said that "Bandura is clearly the intellectual heir of Sears, influenced by but also reacting against the tradition that Sears represented."[7] Yet this tradition was too psychoanalytic, according to Bandura. While Sears sought to reconcile psychoanalysis and behaviorism, Bandura felt that social learning theory should represent a departure from psychoanalysis.

Bandura also drew on the work of Dollard and Miller, who investigated social learning and imitation. Bandura thought that they had interesting ideas around imitation but were too narrow in their scope. They believed that imitation alone was a suitable predictive model for behavior; for Bandura, that model was limited because it did not look at how behavior is created on a social as well as an individual level. Bandura went on to expand on this criticism of Dollard and Miller, and that critique became the basis of his ideas on social learning theory, later developed into social cognitive theory* (a wider theory incorporating the ideas of social learning theory).

NOTES

1   Neal Elgar Miller and John Dollard, *Social Learning and Imitation* (New Haven: Yale University Press, 1941).

2   Albert Bandura and Richard H. Walters, *Adolescent Aggression: A study of the Influence of Child-Training Practices and Family Interrelationships* (New York: Ronald Press 1959).

3   Albert Bandura, "Autobiography," in *A History of Psychology in Autobiography*, vol. 9, eds. M. G. Lindzey and W. M. Runyan (Washington, DC: American Psychological Association, 2007), 42–74.

4   Héfer Bembenutty, "The Last Word: An Interview with Frank Pajares: God, the Devil, William James, the Little Prince, and Self-Efficacy," *Journal of Advanced Academics* 18, no. 4 (2007): 660–77.

5   John Dollard, Neal E. Miller, Leonard W. Doob, Orval Hobart Mowrer, and Robert R. Sears. *Frustration and Aggression* (New Haven, CT: Yale University Press, 1939).

6   Patrik Lindenfors and Birgitta S. Tullberg, "Evolutionary Aspects of Aggression: The Importance of Sexual Selection," *Advances in Genetics* 75 (2011): 7.

    Burphus Frederic Skinner and C. B. Ferster, *Schedules of Reinforcement* (Cambridge, MA: B.F. Skinner Foundation, 2015).

7   Joan E. Grusec, "Social Learning Theory and Developmental Psychology: The Legacies of Robert Sears and Albert Bandura," *Developmental Psychology* 28, no. 5 (1992): 776.

THE PROBLEM

KEY POINTS

- The main question engaging psychologists at the time of *Aggression* was, "Why do humans behave the way that they do?" Albert Bandura was particularly concerned with aggression.

- At the time, the main theories used by psychologists to explain aggression were psychoanalysis,* evolution* and the "frustration-aggression hypothesis"* (according to which aggression was a result of frustration).

- Bandura built upon those viewpoints, ultimately extending the behaviorist* arguments of B. F. Skinner* to social factors.

Core Question

In *Aggression: A Social Learning Analysis* (1973), Albert Bandura wanted to answer the core question of why people behave aggressively. He explores several different facets of that question in the book, among them what was known by researchers at the time about aggression, the origins of aggression, how aggression is instigated, how it is maintained, and what can be done to control and modify aggressive behaviors. He achieves all this by using the framework of social learning theory,* which proposes that people learn not only by directly performing a task but also by means of observation,* imitation,* modeling,* and vicariously* ("second hand") from the environment.

For Bandura, existing theories of aggression had not made enough effort to characterize its causes. He thought that, while aggression had been investigated at the individual level, not enough

> **66** This book is concerned with why man aggresses. **99**
>
> Albert Bandura, *Aggression: A Social Learning Analysis*

attention had been given to expressions of aggression at the level of society. He was particularly concerned about the level of violence portrayed in the media, and he was unhappy with the role played by media companies, stating, "They can think of many reasons why the social effects of television can never be clearly understood."[1]

By this he means that television companies are guilty of distorting the issue of links between violence and its depiction because they are against the regulation or censorship of TV images. Bandura advocates for the study and consideration of empirical* evidence (evidence verifiable by observation) about the effects of violent imagery in the media. He has also been concerned about the destructive power of new technological advances, such as nuclear weapons.

The Participants

The psychoanalytic theory of Sigmund Freud* described aggressive behavior as a "primary response"*—that it arises as a result of other drives being suppressed (mainly the drive to seek pleasure or avoid pain). He later developed his theories of human motivation in a different direction, arguing instead that humans are driven by Eros,* the life instinct, and Thanatos,* the death drive. Aggression, Freud believed, is an innate drive born of the conflict between these two primary motivations—meaning that aggressive behavior is inevitable and unavoidable.

Evolutionary* or "ethological"* accounts of aggression state that humans are all born with the capacity for aggressive behavior as a result of evolutionary development. Bandura's main contemporary in this field was Konrad Lorenz,* who published *On Aggression* in 1966.[2]

Lorenz's main contention, which had some similarities to the psychoanalytic theories of Freud, was that humans have an inborn desire to act aggressively, and the urge to do so builds up until an appropriate occasion for release appears. Lorenz argued that humans are born with an animal-like drive for aggression but without the capacity for more passive behavior seen in, for example, beta* males—males lower down the hierarchical structure in animal communities. Based on this argument, Lorenz also saw human aggression as inevitable.

Before Bandura's work, the "frustration-aggression" hypothesis was the most widely accepted theory of aggression. The theory suggests that aggression arises when a specific goal is blocked or delayed. For example, a child who cannot perform a task as requested may get angry and hit his or her parent. Early iterations of the hypothesis stated, "Aggression is always a consequence of frustration."[3] However, later versions of the same theory disputed this—particularly the work of the psychologist John Dollard,* who argued that there were other responses to frustration. He relied heavily on psychoanalytic principles to explain what prompted aggressive responses.

Another prominent aggression researcher, Leonard Berkowitz,* further expanded these early theories. He has suggested a cognitive neoassociation* model—according to which behavior is associated with conditioned or unconditioned responses—to explain which feelings will elicit certain behaviors: "The experience of fear presumably accompanies the escape/avoidance tendencies and theoretically develops out of the ideas, memories, expressive-motor reactions, and physiological sensations associated with escape/avoidance, whereas the experience of anger theoretically goes along with the aggressive tendencies and is built from aggression-related ideas, memories, expressive-motor responses, and bodily sensations."[4]

In other words, different emotions correspond to different physical effects in the body. These correspondences, Berkowitz has argued, make up a network of behavioral tendencies that certain prompts can activate.

The Contemporary Debate

In *Aggression*, Bandura states of Freud's explanations of human behavior, "In recent years much [simpler]—and empirically verifiable—explanations of why people repeatedly behave in self-injurious ways have been advanced by learning theorists."[5] He also recognizes that empirical* evidence did not support Freud's theories.

Psychology as an academic discipline was somewhat moving away from psychoanalysis at the time when Bandura was writing his book. In this new academic climate, researchers began to object to theories based on subjectivity and case studies, as the new psychology favored objective experimentation and quantitative* measurements (numerical figures such as statistics). Lack of empirical evidence was also one of Bandura's major problems with both the frustration-aggression hypothesis and with Freudian psychoanalysis. As he notes in *Aggression*, "In point of fact, the formula that frustration breeds aggression does not hold up well under empirical scrutiny in laboratory studies."[6]

Similarly Bandura also has major criticisms of Lorenz's theories. His main opposition was that while humans may not have an innate surrender gene as Lorenz had observed in animals, we have something much better: language. "National leaders," he writes, "can therefore better safeguard against catastrophic violence by verbal communiqués than by snapping their teeth or erecting their hair, especially in view of the prevalence of baldness in the higher echelons."[7] Bandura also criticizes the subjective nature of the theories that Lorenz proposed in his book, *On Aggression*, mentioning that other readers of Lorenz's work had similar concerns.

NOTES

1 Albert Bandura, *Aggression: A Social Learning Analysis*, Prentice-Hall Series in Social Learning Theory (New Jersey: Prentice-Hall Englewood Cliffs, 1973), 218.

2 Lorenz Konrad, *On Aggression* (New York/London: Routledge 2002).

3 John Dollard, Neal E. Miller, Leonard W. Doob, Orval Hobart Mowrer, and Robert R. Sears, *Frustration and Aggression* (New Haven, CT: Yale University Press, 1939).

4 Leonard Berkowitz, "Frustration-Aggression Hypothesis: Examination and Reformulation," *Psychological Bulletin* 106, no. 1 (1989): 59.

5 Bandura, *Aggression*, 13.

6 Bandura, *Aggression*, 32.

7 Bandura, *Aggression*, 16.

MODULE 4
THE AUTHOR'S CONTRIBUTION

KEY POINTS

- Bandura argued that human aggression is due to socialization*—the process by which we learn to interact with our social environment—and he used social learning theory* to explain this process.

- Social learning theory states that behavior is learned through observation,* modeling,* and copying.*

- These theories were initially developed from B. F. Skinner's* behaviorist* models—animal experiments designed to show that behavior can be explained entirely by external causes. They refuted existing theories of aggression based on drives and instincts.

Author's Aims

Albert Bandura's main aims for *Aggression: A Social Learning Analysis* are laid out in the preface to the book. The first sentence broadly and succinctly defines its purpose: "This book is concerned with why man aggresses."[1] Bandura recognized the changing state of the world and the huge technological advances in human destructive capabilities. He felt that it was more necessary than ever to build solid foundations to the understanding of aggression and its causes. Bandura's earlier work on imitation with his doctoral student at the time, Richard Walters, set the scene for "the power of social modeling"[2] by examining adolescent aggression, particularly in privileged teenaged boys.[3]

He expands on this work in *Aggression*, where he "attempted to formulate a social learning theory of aggression sufficiently broad in scope to integrate evidence on all facets."[4] In this, he was looking to analyze everything about aggressive behavior.

> 66 Although aggression pervades our lives, few concerted efforts have been made to substantiate its causes or to devise constructive ways of reducing the level of societal violence. 99
>
> Albert Bandura, *Aggression: A Social Learning Analysis.*

Bandura divides *Aggression* into five sections, with a clear line of argument throughout. In the first chapter, he aims to explain theories and definitions of aggression. The second chapter explores the origins of aggression. The third and fourth chapters debate the causes of aggression and the conditions that maintain it. Finally, in chapter five, Bandura suggests how aggression might be modified and controlled. He compiles the text from a number of sources across several decades and builds on and analyzes past and current ideas about aggression.

Approach

Bandura set out to examine aggression both at an individual and collective level. He wanted the book to "offer a better basis for explaining, predicting and modifying aggression ... to provide impetus for new lines of research likely to augment the explanatory power of social learning theory."[5] In other words, he hoped that the book would inspire others to expand on his ideas.

In it, he approaches the question of why humans behave aggressively by examining their behavior both through the lens of the theory of social learning* and by analyzing and critiquing other theories. He argues that social learning theory is a more successful predictive model for explaining aggressive behavior than previous theories, including evolutionary* explanations, psychoanalytic* arguments, and the frustration–aggression hypothesis.*

The originality of Bandura's approach lies in the social learning perspective he uses to analyze aggression. He extends existing ideas concerning imitation from Neal Miller* and John Dollard,* who stated that "imitation can greatly hasten the process of independent learning by enabling the subject to perform the first correct response sooner than he otherwise would."[6] The concept of imitation, then, was already a hallmark of social learning theory when Bandura wrote *Aggression*. Bandura builds on this, greatly expanding the theoretical concept of social learning that scholars at Yale University developed under the direction of Mark May* and other psychologists such as Julian Rotter.*

Rotter was known for his work developing the "locus of control"* theory, which describes the degree of control that a person feels that her or she has over events. In his book, Bandura also discusses self-regulation* (the ability to control your own behavior), and self-efficacy* (the way in which a person approaches goals and challenges) in relation to aggression. This approach—foregrounding an individual's ability to make independent choices—was contrary to most theories at the time. They stated that human behavior was essentially an unconscious* process—that is, it was not controlled by thinking alone and so not a matter of choice.

Bandura uses aggression as a context in which to explore social learning theory, which he later renamed social cognitive theory. Social cognitive theory is a framework for describing the interplay between the environment, cognition,* and behavior, and it proposes that behavior is learned through observation, imitation, and modeling. In *Aggression*, Bandura contends not only that our environment (such as families, peers and symbolic aspects such as the media) influences our behavior but also that our cognition has an effect on our environment. He calls this two-way relationship between environment and cognition "reciprocal determination."*

Contribution in Context
Bandura's writings on aggression from a perspective of social learning theory became seminal in the discipline of psychology. His work

provided a more complete framework than any other hypothesis for explaining aggression in a myriad of situations. In the book, Bandura manages to combine the ideas of imitation, observation, and modeling with aspects of reinforcement* (learning through reward and punishment) and other behaviorist principles.

However, he widens the definitions of modeling and reinforcement in new ways. He also proposes that a person has various opportunities to see or experience modeled behavior, all of which can affect his or her cognitive response. People later referred to this as the agentic* concept, according to which humans, having cognitive agency (the ability to make independent action in terms of thought), do not just respond to instinct and drives: we are both thinking and feeling creatures.

Bandura's work on aggression helped to build a literature and "conversation" around social learning theory.[7] His integration of the fields of cognitive, behavioral, and social psychology, and his use of experimental methodology, marked a new type of psychology. *Aggression* extended behaviorism further into human action from its origins in experiments based on animals, and it applied the concept of cognition to social behavior. It united many threads of psychological research that had never been brought together before.

NOTES

1   Albert Bandura, *Aggression: A Social Learning Analysis*, Prentice-Hall Series in Social Learning Theory (New Jersey: Prentice-Hall Englewood Cliffs, 1973), 7.

2   Albert Bandura, "Autobiography," in *A History of Psychology in Autobiography*, vol. 9, eds. M. G. Lindzey and W. M. Runyan (Washington, DC.: American Psychological Association, 2007), 42–74.

3   Albert Bandura, Richard H. Walters, and Robert R. Sears, *Adolescent Aggression* (New York: Ronald Press, 1959).

4   Bandura, *Aggression*, 8.

5   Bandura, *Aggression*, 8.

6   Neal Edgar Miller and John Dollard, *Social Learning and Imitation* (New Haven: Yale University Press), 221.

7   Barry J. Zimmerman and Dale H. Schunk, "Albert Bandura: The Man and His Contributions to Educational Psychology," in *Educational Psychology: One-Hundred Years of Contributions* (New Jersey: Lawrence Earlbaum, 2003), 431–57.

SECTION 2
IDEAS

MAIN IDEAS

KEY POINTS

- Albert Bandura argues that the framework of social learning theory* — the theory that behavior is caused by learning through observation, imitation, and modeling—can explain why humans behave aggressively.

- Bandura divides his book into five chapters, each dealing with a different aspect of aggressive behavior. The first chapter describes theories of aggression; the second looks at the origins of aggression; the third chapter concerns the instigators or triggers of aggression; the fourth outlines the "maintaining conditions" or the conditions that sustain and develop aggression, and the fifth and final chapter examines the modification and control of aggression.

- While Bandura intended the book to be accessible to a wide audience of readers, he also targeted his arguments at the scientific community, providing a new scientific perspective on aggression through his famous Bobo doll experiments* (which used an inflatable toy to study the behavior of children).

Key Themes

The main theme of Albert Bandura's *Aggression: A Social Learning Analysis* is that aggression is a behavior learned through the social processes of imitation,* observation,* and modeling.* This was a radical departure from prominent theories regarding aggression at the time, which argued that behavior was due to drives or instincts that were not within full control of individuals.

> 66 In short, people do not have to be angered or emotionally aroused to behave aggressively. A culture can produce highly aggressive people, while keeping frustration at a low level, by valuing aggressive accomplishments, furnishing successful aggressive models, and ensuring that aggressive actions secure rewarding effects. 99
>
> Albert Bandura, *Aggression: A Social Learning Analysis*

Aggression's five chapters cover five main themes. The first chapter focuses on existing research and theories on aggression; it offers a definition of what aggression is and examines the theoretical background of aggression as a concept. This chapter covers Freudian* and psychoanalytic* explanations (theories of behavior based on drives and inner conflicts), evolutionary* or ethological* theories (theories of behavior based on instincts to survive and reproduce), and drive theories,* such as the frustration–aggression hypothesis* (theories based on the conflict between our intentions and outcomes). This chapter then goes on to explain Bandura's social learning theory, which is the major thread of the book's overall argument: that behavior can be explained through the learning processes of observation, imitation, and modeling.

The second chapter, "Origins of Aggression," explains how aggression is a behavior learned though modeling, practice, or under other naturally occurring conditions—that is, those that can be found outside experimental contexts. In the third chapter, the book then goes on to discuss instigators (that is, triggers) of aggression and also explores modeling, along with other issues such as aversive treatment (how bad treatment by others can influence the development of aggression in an individual).

In the fourth chapter, Bandura studies the conditions that maintain aggressive behavior. He does this mostly from a behaviorist* viewpoint—the view that behavior can be entirely explained by external causes—looking at different forms of reinforcement* and punishment.* He also touches briefly on collective aggression,* or aggressive behavior from a number of people together. Finally, the fifth chapter looks at modifying and controlling aggression, arguing that this is made possible by understanding the principles of social learning and using them to reduce aggressive behavior.

Exploring the Ideas

Aggression's main claim is that social learning theory answers the question of why people are aggressive. According to Bandura, "Virtually, all learning phenomena resulting from direct experience can occur on a vicarious basis through observation of other people's behavior and its consequences."[1] By this he means that children can learn by watching how people react to the behavior of others. Once patterns of behavior have been established, Bandura explains, regulatory functions*— mechanisms that reproduce and maintain certain habits in an individual or society—reinforce them. "Human aggression is a learned construct that, like other forms of social behavior, is under stimulus,* reinforcement and cognitive control," he argues. Bandura explains stimulus control: "When behaving like others produces rewarding outcomes, modeling cues become powerful determinants of analogous behavior."[2]

In other words, if a child is rewarded for behaving in a particular way he is likely to continue behaving in that manner. If, however, he is punished, he is likely to try to avoid behaving that way in the future. Bandura goes on to say of reinforcement control, "As a result of repeated association with primary experiences, social reactions in the form of verbal approval, reprimands, attention, affection, and rejection acquire powerful reinforcing functions." Our social world forms the basis on which we learn how to behave, and many aspects of socialization*—the process by which we learn to interact with our social environment—can act as positive reinforcement or negative punishment. Through understanding how others will likely receive our behavior, we form our own patterns of action.

Bandura goes on to explain the role of cognition* (the working processes of the brain that enable us to learn about and understand our environment.) and how it interacts with other principles. For example, memory is a cognitive process about which Bandura writes, "The memory trace of momentary influences is short lived, but such experiences often have lasting behavioral effects."[3] In other words, if a reaction to a behavior is significantly positive or negative, then it is likely to be remembered well and therefore be either repeated (if the reaction is positive) or avoided (if it is negative). Bandura also explains that acts are often rehearsed in the mind, that those thoughts act as their own reinforcement, and that cognitive events such as this interact with learned actions to produce human behavior.

Language and Expression

One of *Aggression*'s aims was to bring the use of the scientific method in psychology to a broader audience. Bandura's text is relatively free of jargon and easy to read, and its ideas are illustrated with examples. This makes understanding his theoretical suggestions relatively straightforward for most levels of learners. He describes the Bobo doll experiments,* for example, in some detail.

As Bandura explains, a Bobo doll is an inflatable toy made of vinyl or plastic, usually about five feet tall, with a weighted base so that if someone hits or pushes it, it comes back to its original position. Bandura's Bobo doll experiments involved nursery-school children in the following situations:

- Witnessing no aggression toward the Bobo doll
- Watching an adult of the same or a different gender behaving aggressively toward the doll
- Watching a video of an adult of the same or a different gender behaving aggressively toward the doll
- Watching a cartoon depicting violence toward the Bobo doll

Following that, researchers put children in the same room as a Bobo doll and then observed and recorded their behavior. They were looking for aggressive acts towards the doll, such as punching or kicking it. The results showed that watching an adult attack the doll produced the most imitation: the children who witnessed a person in front of them behaving aggressively to the Bobo doll were the most likely to do the same. The second most likely situation to produce aggressive behavior was the video condition, in which children watched a video of an adult attacking the doll.

The third most likely was the cartoon condition, in which children watched a cartoon depicting violence toward the doll. Interestingly, however, Bandura found that the opposite was true for increasing *overall* aggression: those in the cartoon conditions were less likely to aggress directly towards the Bobo doll, but they were more likely to throw or hit other toys or say aggressive things.

The study's results, Bandura states, "show that exposure to aggressive models had two important effects on viewers. First it taught them new ways of aggressing. Most of the children who had observed the aggressive models later emulated their novel assaultive behavior and hostile remarks … The children were less inclined however, to imitate the cartoon character than the real-life model."[4] He argues that this was because, while the cartoon represented a fictional character that the children could not relate to directly, the aggressive tone of the program still influenced them. Hence their aggression was general and not just directed at the doll.

The Bobo doll experiments set the bar for aggression research and were widely received as groundbreaking in terms of social learning theory.

NOTES

1   Albert Bandura, *Aggression: A Social Learning Analysis*, Prentice-Hall Series in Social Learning Theory (New Jersey: Prentice-Hall Englewood Cliffs, 1973), 12.

2   Bandura, *Aggression*, 13.

3   Bandura, *Aggression*, 52.

4   Bandura, *Aggression*, 74.

MODULE 6
SECONDARY IDEAS

KEY POINTS

- One of Albert Bandura's most important ideas was that observing depictions of violence in the media can promote real violence elsewhere in society.

- Bandura was a major proponent of using scientific methods to demonstrate the principles of social learning as the radical behaviorists had done before with animal experiments.

- Bandura also suggested that reinforcement*—positive or negative feedback—maintained aggression in individuals.

Other Ideas

One of the most interesting propositions of Albert Bandura's *Aggression: A Social Learning Analysis* is that representations of violence in the media could act as reinforcement for aggressive behavior. As he states, "It might be noted here that assassins in some of the sensational mass slayings originally got the idea from reports of a mass killing. The incident remained salient in their thinking long after it had been forgotten by others, and it was repeatedly revivified and elaborated until, under appropriate instigating conditions, it served as the basis for an analogous murderous action."[1]

It is not just real acts of violence that Bandura is concerned with— he also states that fictional depictions of aggression can act as reinforcement. He provides data showing that viewing television violence in childhood leads to increased aggression 10 years later.

One of Bandura's distinctive theories was that reinforcement can act as a maintaining force for aggressive behavior. If a child is rewarded in

> **❝** Exposure to modeled violence presented in ways that legitimize its use not only raises the probability of aggressive conduct, but also tends to increase preference for aggressive toys, stressful mood states and selection of aggressive solutions to depicted conflicts. **❞**
>
> Albert Bandura, *Aggression: A Social Learning Analysis*

some way for behaving aggressively (if he or she finds that aggressive behavior helps get his or her parents' attention, for example), then they are likely to repeat that type of behavior—in fact, it may even become habitual. Bandura states that aggressive individuals possess "a *self*-reinforcement system in which aggressive actions are a source of personal pride." He also departs from previous theory by stating that emotional arousal of any kind may cause aggression if it is cognitively experienced as frustration or anger or some other cue likely to cause aggression.

Exploring the Ideas

Bandura's use of empirical* methods to support his theoretical standpoint is very important. Most social psychology research up to that point was still concerned with the largely subjective underpinnings of psychoanalysis.* Even other social learning theorists such as Neal Miller* and John Dollard* attempted to integrate psychoanalytic theory into their arguments regarding aggressive behavior.

Aggression was also one of the first works to use experimental methodologies from the outset to refute psychoanalytic arguments. For example, people theorized that an aggressive act would provide catharsis*—a moment of emotional release—and relieve pent up energy. Early child therapists would therefore actually encourage children to behave extra aggressively. They called this "performance catharsis,"* with the idea that, once this energy was released, the child would feel more calm.

Bandura uses other research to refute that practice, stating, "Evidence from research studies of children indicates that, far from producing a cathartic reduction of aggression, participation in aggressive activities within a permissive setting maintains the behavior at its original level or actually increases it."[2] Bandura also contends that the reinforcement of aggressive behavior can be positive, which was a departure from earlier theories that suggested that aggression was always produced by a negative internal drive.

Overlooked

A less-developed idea in Albert Bandura's *Aggression* is the link between age, development, and aggression. Much research in the 1970s centered on child development but neglected those links. A reviewer describing the impact of Bandura's work said that his social cognitive theory* "began to be criticized for its lack of attention to the importance of changes with age that might have an impact on behavior."[3] This omission by Bandura may be because research into age and observational learning was relatively young at the time of his writing.[4]

Another area that does not receive a great deal of attention in the text is the weighting that Bandura had assigned to different elements of the dynamic interplay between aggressive behaviors, cognitive factors, and the environment. He places great importance on the role of observational learning but does not discuss weighting determinates* of aggression—that is, on what made one aspect of aggression more important than another.

Additionally, he only briefly touches on the biological and genetic nature of aggression,[5] a topic that has become increasingly important because of scientific developments in brain imaging* (which can be used to see which parts of the brain are active while certain kinds of behavior are exhibited) and genome mapping.* (The latter practice involves recording sequences of genes—the biological material by which inherited characteristics are passed from generation to generation—usually so as to investigate which genes are responsible for illness.)

NOTES

1   Albert Bandura, *Aggression: A Social Learning Analysis*, Prentice-Hall Series in Social Learning Theory (New Jersey: Prentice-Hall Englewood Cliffs, 1973), 77.

2   Bandura, *Aggression*, 148.

3   Joan E. Grusec, "Social Learning Theory and Developmental Psychology: The Legacies of Robert Sears and Albert Bandura," *Developmental Psychology* 28, no.5 (1992): 784.

4   Brian Coates, and Willard W. Hartup, "Age and Verbalization in Observational Learning," *Developmental Psychology* 1, no. 5 (1969): 556.

5   C. Ray Jefferey, "Criminology as an Interdisciplinary Behavioral Science," *Criminology* 16, no. 2 (1978): 149–69.

MODULE 7
ACHIEVEMENT

KEY POINTS

- Albert Bandura successfully described aggressive behavior from the perspective of social learning theory:* the idea that behavior is learned through social processes.

- His use of empirical* evidence and the scientific method, in contrast to subjective theories of behavior, contributed to the work's success.

- Although the work was well received, people generally had some methodological and ethical concerns regarding how Bandura conducted his research.

Assessing the Argument

In *Aggression: A Social Learning Analysis*, Albert Bandura introduced a new version of social learning theory in the context of aggression. His arguments were immediately relevant to an audience that extended from the academic world to practical professions like teaching. One of Bandura's goals, which he succeeded in meeting, was to create new lines of research.

A critical analysis highlighted the significance of his work, stating, "By reading Bandura's original writings … readers have no doubt become aware that research needs to be done on imitating media presentations of the corollary of aggression: pro-social behaviors. One begins to wonder if there are indeed too few examples of this type of behavior in the media to merit investigation or if there is an obsession with the problem rather than seeking prospective solutions."[1]

> ❝ Social learning theory has evolved over the years in a way that is responsive to new data. ❞
>
> Joan E. Grusec, "Social Learning Theory and Developmental Psychology: The Legacies of Robert Sears and Albert Bandura"

In this sense, although Bandura had highlighted the problems of depictions of violence in the media, the field needed to be expanded to understand how the media could inspire more positive behaviors.

However, since the publication of *Aggression*, the severity and frequency of depictions of violence in many forms of media, both new and old has increased.[2] This means that Bandura's research into aggression is of great relevance to today's society. The theoretical foundations that he laid down about the ways that we learn, maintain, and control aggression as a society are still highly pertinent today.

Achievement in Context

Broadly speaking, *Aggression* achieves its aims. Bandura successfully reviewed the current state of the field, looking at the causes of aggression and presenting ideas for its control. One reviewer contended that "at times the author strays from the path of scholarly rigor into the polemic thicket."[3] He criticized Bandura for being overly broad and taking sides in his arguments, and not being academic enough. This criticism could be seen as unfair, as Bandura stated from the beginning that he wanted the work to appeal to a broad audience rather than just an academic one. Despite this, *Aggression* primarily presents empirical evidence that one can test scientifically.*

Although Bandura's criticism of other theories of behavior is confrontational, this may have stimulated further debate regarding psychoanalysis and evolution. Bandura emphasized social learning theory rather than competing views, such as performance catharsis* (according to which performing an act will release the pressure of struggling *not* to perform that act),[4] but that bias is to be expected. The effect of the media on behavior is still hotly debated, despite a growing body of increasing evidence that supports Bandura's theory.[5]

Bandura wrote for a broad audience about individual aggression, aggression in society, and in institutions. The book is accessible and relevant to many disciplines, not only that of psychology. Aggression and social learning theories have come to touch almost every aspect of society. An indication of the success of this text is that that people are still debating it and citing it in articles and books in many different subject areas.

Limitations

One reviewer criticized the empirical nature of *Aggression*: "Sociologists, who recall the problems in the application of laboratory findings on persuasion to attitude changes in non-experimental settings, might do well to suspect the generalizability of Bandura's model."[6] The reviewer is questioning the ecological validity* of Bandura's approach (the extent to which laboratory experiments really help us find out how people behave in the real world). This was not a new problem in social science, and scholars are still debating it.

Although many people see Bandura's Bobo doll experiments* as a great example of taking the outside world into the laboratory in a meaningful way, others criticize how the experiments were performed. They raise ethical objections to involving children in the experiments and make accusations of bias in the design of the experiments.[7] Some scholars have argued that Bobo dolls are in fact toys designed to be punched and kicked and therefore not appropriate tools to measure aggression. However, the results in the cartoon condition, which showed that even depictions of aggressive behavior toward the doll in a cartoon increased real-life aggressive behavior overall, may provide evidence to refute this.

It must also be remembered that ethical criticisms of earlier research based on the standards and knowledge of today is not necessarily fair. By modern standards, many well-respected psychology institutions were indulging in a great number of ethically dubious experiments back when Bandura was researching and writing *Aggression*. The Milgram* experiments (in which participants were led to believe they were delivering potentially fatal electric shocks) and the Zimbardo* experiment (in which a group of students were subjected to a simulation of prison) were other experiments which, while raising eyebrows at the time, were still applauded for their ingenuity. Today's criticism of Bandura's research may be partly due to heightened ethical standards, particularly around the use of children in experiments.

NOTES

1   Karen E. Hart, F. Scholar, W. A. Kristonis, and D. Alumnus, "Critical Analysis of an Original Writing on Social Learning Theory: Imitation of Film-Mediated Aggressive Models By: Albert Bandura, Dorothea Ross and Sheila A. Ross," *National Forum of Applied Educational Research Journal*, vol. 20, no. 3. (2006): 7.

2   Christopher J. Ferguson, *Adolescents, Crime, and the Media: A Critical Analysis* (New York: Springer, 2013), 83–104.

3   Alan C. Kerckhoff, "Review: *Aggression: A Social Learning Analysis*, by Albert Bandura," *American Journal of Sociology* 80, no. 1 (1974): 250.

4   Seymour Feshbach and Robert D. Singer, *Television and Aggression: An Experimental Field Study* (Jossey-Bass: San Francisco, 1971).

5   Jennifer E. Lansford, "Beyond Bandura's Bobo Doll Studies," in *Developmental Psychology: Revisiting the Classic Studies*, eds. Alan M. Slater and Paul C. Quinn (London: SAGE, 2012), 176.

6   John C. Touhey, "Review: *Aggression: A Social Learning Analysis* by Albert Bandura," *Contemporary Sociology* 4, no. 2 (1975): 170.

7   Hart, Scholar, et al, "Critical Analysis," 4.

MODULE 8
PLACE IN THE AUTHOR'S WORK

KEY POINTS

- *Aggression: A Social Learning Analysis* came early in Albert Bandura's career. He continued to publish works on aggression and develop his social learning theory.

- The book is among his most important and cited works.

- Bandura still publishes on the subject of social psychology,* particularly around self-efficacy* (an individual's belief that they can deal with situations) and self-regulation (an individual's ability to control their own behavior).*

Positioning

Albert Bandura's publications span over half a century, from the 1950s to the present. In 1973, he published *Aggression: A Social Learning Analysis*, which effectively reviewed the then current state of aggression research and placed a new emphasis, using empirical findings, on social learning theory.* After its publication, Bandura continued to publish work on the topic of aggression.

Bandura extended the ideas he first developed in *Aggression* to address the subject of terrorism, beginning in 1978 at a talk at Stanford University. While he thought that morality could help to regulate and control societies, he also recognized that "moral standards do not function as fixed internal regulators of conduct. Self-regulatory mechanisms do not operate unless they are activated, and there are many psychological processes by which moral reactions can be disengaged from inhumane conduct."[1] In other words, people who commit acts of terrorism may feel that their actions are justified

> ❝One morning, I was wasting time in the library. Someone had forgotten to return a course catalog, and I thumbed through it attempting to find a filler course to occupy the early time slot. I noticed a course in psychology that would serve as excellent filler. It sparked my interest and I found my career.❞
>
> Albert Bandura, *Autobiography*

according to a different moral standard or because they do not make a link between moral standards and their own behavior.

Later, Bandura argued that the media may play a role in influencing terrorism, just as it does with interpersonal violence: "Terrorists try to exercise influence over targeted officials or nations through intimidation of the public and arousal of sympathy for the social and political causes they espouse. Without widespread publicity, terrorist acts can achieve neither of these effects."[2]

Turning his attention to more positive aspects of human action, Bandura has also written numerous books and articles on self-regulation[3] and self-efficacy—ways that people can control their own behavior.[4]

Integration

After the publication of *Aggression*, Bandura worked on developing his social learning theory. By studying the way in which children learn aggression and their interactions with society, he later widened the scope of his research to encompass learning as a whole. He sought to understand how people self-regulate (that is, how they successfully control their own behavior), extensively developing this idea later in his career.[5]

Regarding self-regulation, Bandura argues that one can effectively self-manage through the three social processes of "self-monitoring of one's behavior, its determinants, and its effects; judgment of one's behavior in relation to personal standards and environmental circumstances; and affective self-reaction."[6] In other words, we can manage our own behavior through observing our own actions, comparing ourself to others around us, and reflecting on the consequences of our behavior.

Of self-efficacy, Bandura writes, "Expectations of personal efficacy determine whether coping behavior will be initiated, how much effort will be expended, and how long it will be sustained in the face of obstacles and aversive experiences."[7]

An individual's existing idea of his or her personal capacities influences how he or she behaves in new situations. Bandura believed that all psychological treatments should work on the principle of increasing one's ability or one's belief in one's ability to cope in the world.

His main ideas have followed a logical progression of thought, beginning with the study of aggression, self-efficacy, and self-regulation. Bandura started his career investigating what makes people destructive and has spent the later part of his career studying self-control. His work in this latter area has also been seminal.

Significance

Although Albert Bandura was already known for his earlier work on aggression before the publication of *Aggression*, the book solidified his reputation as a key thinker in the field of psychology. It was one of the first well-rounded applications of social learning theory to a particular behavior. Its sympathetic but acute criticism of previous theories also helped establish Bandura's skills as a critical analyst. His well-received arguments regarding the need to depart from psychoanalysis as the primary explanatory framework for behavior were important in the general shift to a new school of psychology. This new school gained importance in every other psychological discipline including forensic psychology, psychotherapy, and studies of memory, and it remains important today.

Bandura's criticism of media violence has also had wide-reaching implications. He was among the first scholars to not only openly criticize the media but also to produce and highlight empirical evidence demonstrating that watching depictions of violence in the media has a direct and lasting effect on later behavior. Although people have criticized him heavily for this, he has refused to change his position on any of his statements.

More-recent events such as the Columbine massacre* (a school shooting committed at Columbine high school in Colorado, USA, in 1999) or the cinema shootings in Aurora,* Colorado, in 2012) have been linked to the influence of depictions of violence in the media, recalling Bandura's reporting on the impact of violent news imagery on mass killers in the 1960s. Bandura's warnings about the effects of reporting on these events have not been followed, however, regardless of their relevance.[8]

NOTES

1   Albert Bandura, "Mechanisms of Moral Disengagement in Terrorism." *Origins of Terrorism: Psychologies, Ideologies, States of Mind* (1990): 161–191.

2   Albert Bandura, "Mechanisms," 161–191.

3   Albert Bandura and Forest J. Jourden, "Self-Regulatory Mechanisms Governing the Impact of Social Comparison on Complex Decision Making," *Journal of Personality and Social Psychology* 60, no. 6 (1991): 941–51.

4   Albert Bandura, *Self-Efficacy: The Exercise of Control* (New York: W.H Freeman and Company, 1997).

5   Barry J. Zimmerman and Dale H. Schunk, "Albert Bandura: The Man and His Contributions to Educational Psychology," in *Educational Psychology: One Hundred Years of Contributions* (New Jersey: Lawrence Earlbaum, 2003).

6   Albert Bandura, "Social Cognitive Theory of Self-Regulation," *Organizational Behavior and Human Decision Processes* 50, no. 2 (1991): 248–287.

7   Albert Bandura, "Self-Efficacy: Toward a Unifying Theory of Behavioral Change," *Psychological Review* 84, no. 2 (1977): 191.

8   See, e.g., http://www.huffingtonpost.com/2013/09/17/columbine-dave-cullen-mass-shootings_n_3943713.html.

SECTION 3
IMPACT

THE FIRST RESPONSES

KEY POINTS

- People criticized Albert Bandura's theoretical standpoint for using laboratory experiments to explain naturalistic behavior* (behavior that occurs in the real world in ways that might be different from experimental conditions).

- He was also criticized for being unethical in his use of children in his experiments and, according to his critics, teaching them aggression.

- For Bandura's part, he attacked the media for its portrayals of violence, which prompted a backlash from some people.

Criticism

While Albert Bandura's *Aggression: A Social Learning Analysis* was popular and influential on the whole, there were some criticisms of the work. One reviewer, working in sociology, commented, "I doubt that social policy can be formulated on the basis of laboratory findings."[1] One of the main criticisms of laboratory research in the social sciences is that results may not be applicable in a real-world situation and that laboratory research lacks a naturalistic standpoint.[2]

Similarly, others suggested that Bandura did not investigate naturally occurring aggression rigorously enough. Though he did include a section on this subject in the book, one reviewer said, "While psychology's recent concern with relevance is most laudable, I do not think we can expect many insights into social problems from psychological approaches that abuse sociology in this fashion."[3] Such critics thought Bandura was jumping to conclusions in his research. His writing style also prompted criticism, with one reviewer stating, "At times [he] strays from the path of scholarly rigor."[4]

> ❝ One evening I received a call from one of my graduate students telling me to turn on my television set to see the character playing my role undergoing a blistering cross-examination concerning my modeling studies. I wasn't doing too well! ❞
>
> Albert Bandura, *Autobiography*

One line of attack of Bandura's aggression work centered on the aspects of behavior that his modeling theory did not seem to address. "Critics argued that modeling cannot build cognitive* skills because thought processes are covert." As cognitive processes occur inside a person's mind, they are not observable and, therefore, not testable. Additionally, advocates of genetic and biological theories, which see aggression as an autonomic response to certain situations, have found fault with the concept of social learning as the main framework for understanding aggression.[5] When *Aggression* was published, however, these theories were in their infancy.

Although Bandura's view of observational modeling*—learning from the people around us—became widely accepted, the most controversial debates occurred between Bandura and television producers. As Alan C. Kerckhoff wrote in an early review, Bandura attacks "the television industry and its underlying morality."[6]

Understandably, television companies took a stance against this. They used the psychoanalytic concept of catharsis* to argue that watching images of aggression releases emotions in the observer and will therefore *reduce* their aggressive tendencies. Some TV companies made satirical programs based on their criticisms of Bandura.[7]

Responses

Regarding criticisms related to the problem of externally testing internal cognitive processes, Bandura responded, "This was a limitation of conceptual vision rather than an inherent limitation of modeling. In fact, cognitive skills can be readily promoted by verbal modeling, in which models verbalize aloud their reasoning strategies ... The thoughts ... are thus made observable and acquirable."[8] In other words, internal cognitive processes can become measurable if someone speaks their thoughts out loud. Bandura further argued that not being able to measure something is not a limitation of the theory—just of the ability to prove it.

Criticisms involving the ecological validity* of measuring behavior in an experimental way—the relevance of laboratory results to real-life contexts—have been made against social psychology as a whole and are still debated today. However, the laboratory-based approach, as the child development scholar Joan Grusec* explains, was seen by many people as a "giant step forward in making the study of social development a truly scientific undertaking."[9]

Most criticisms of the experimental nature of Bandura's research came from people in the discipline of sociology rather than psychology. Other readers applauded Bandura's contribution. One said that "the social learning position strikes me as having wide heuristic value. From where I stand, it certainly would be recommended reading for those who are looking for clues on how to live together more peaceably."[10] This praise also reflects well on Bandura's writing style, which aimed not only "to provide impetus for new lines of research"[11] and inspire debate but also to create a work that people without academic training could understand.

Arguments about the effect of media representations of violence continue. As one reviewer put it, "With respect to television violence, as a case in point, rhetoric has simply engulfed evidence, and each school of thought has hardened into a party line."[12] Bandura's supporters argue that the media have ignored his theories because it has an interest in preventing the regulation and control of images.

Meanwhile, Bandura has maintained his views on the link between aggression and violent imagery on television.

Conflict and Consensus

The element of Bandura's work that has consistently received the most criticism, as well as acclaim, was the involvement of children in his Bobo doll experiments: a set of experiments that helped to lead Bandura to his theory that behavior is learned by watching others. Under controlled conditions, he arranged for groups of children to watch an adult behaving aggressively towards a toy called a Bobo doll* (an inflatable five-foot figure weighted at the bottom so that it returned to the same position when punched or kicked). Another group of children was exposed to a nonaggressive role model, and a control group was not exposed to any role model.

Bandura first performed this experiment with live adults as role models; later he used video of adults performing the aggressive tasks. His experimental design has been critiqued as biased in several respects, including the nature of the Bobo doll (it is designed to be hit), how the modeling was performed, and the selection of the children involved. The main concerns, however, have related to the ethics of the experiments. Bandura has been accused of "teaching" children to be violent.[13]

Some critics have attacked Bandura's ideas because of what they see as failings in the discipline of psychology. One sociologist criticizes *Aggression* for not being sufficiently sociological, though he admits, "in all fairness, it should be noted that the author is not a sociologist."[14] Despite such criticisms, cognitive theories of aggression and the social learning model are now widely accepted by many psychologists.[15]

NOTES

1   John C. Touhey, "Review: *Aggression: A Social Learning Analysis* by Albert Bandura," *Contemporary Sociology* 4, no. 2 (1975): 171.

2   Urie Bronfenbrenner, "Toward an Experimental Ecology of Human Development," *American Psychologist* 32, no. 7 (1977): 513–31.

3   Touhey, "Review," 171.

4   Alan C. Kerckhoff, "Review: *Aggression: A Social Learning Analysis*, by Albert Bandura," *American Journal of Sociology* 80, no. 1 (1974): 250.

5   C. Ray Jefferey, "Criminology as an Interdisciplinary Behavioral Science," *Criminology* 16, no. 2 (1978): 149–69.

6   Kerckhoff, "Review," 250.

7   Seymour Feshbach and Robert D. Singer, *Television and Aggression: An Experimental Field Study* (Jossey-Bass: San Francisco, 1971).

8   Albert Bandura, "Autobiography," in *A History of Psychology in Autobiography*, vol. 9, eds. M. G. Lindzey and W. M. Runyan (Washington, DC: American Psychological Association, 2007), 42–74.

9   Joan E. Grusec, "Social Learning Theory and Developmental Psychology: The Legacies of Robert Sears and Albert Bandura," *Developmental Psychology* 28, no. 5 (1992): 784.

10 James M. Campbell, "Book Reviews: No Peace in Our Time? Review of *Aggression: A Social Learning Analysis*, by Albert Bandura," *Criminal Justice and Behavior* 2, no. 91 (1975): 93.

11 Albert Bandura, *Aggression: A Social Learning Analysis*, Prentice-Hall Series in Social Learning Theory (New Jersey: Prentice-Hall Englewood Cliffs, 1973), 8.

12 John C. Touhey, "Review of *Aggression: A Social Learning Analysis* by Albert Bandura," Contemporary Sociology 4, no. 2 (1975): 170.

13 Stål Bjørkly, "Psychological Theories of Aggression: Principles and Application to Practice," in *Violence in Mental Health Settings*, ed. Dirk Richter and Richard Whittington (New York: Springer, 2006): 27–46.

14 Touhey, "Review of *Aggression*," 170.

15 Grusec, "Social Learning Theory," 776–85.

THE EVOLVING DEBATE

KEY POINTS

- Albert Bandura's work evolved from social learning theory,* which understood behavior as learned through social processes, to social cognitive theory, which added more cognitive (thought-based) elements to social learning theory, and to self-efficacy and self-control, which concerned people's capacity and belief in their own ability to deal with their circumstances.

- Bandura's work influenced virtually every school of thought in the field of psychology.*

- *Aggression* had a massive impact on the psychology community—not only in terms of shifting social psychology* towards recognizing cognition as important, but also towards a greater use of the scientific method.

Uses and Problems

The main school of thought that evolved from Albert Bandura's seminal text *Aggression: A Social Learning Analysis*, was social learning theory,* the idea that behavior is learned through social processes—which Bandura developed and renamed social cognitive theory* later in his career. Scholars in various fields have used these theories to investigate the social basis for human behavior and decision-making.

Because of the broad applications and impact across multiple fields of Bandura's work, it would be difficult to list the names of everyone whom he has inspired. As a whole, Bandura has brought questions of social learning and self-efficacy to the forefront of psychology. The scholars Craig A. Anderson* and Brad J. Bushman,*

> **❝** Professor Bandura charts the waters I navigate. Without him I would be lost at sea **❞**
>
> Frank Pajares, quoted in Héfer Bembenutty, "The Last Word: An Interview With Frank Pajares: God, the Devil, William James, the Little Prince, and Self-Efficacy"

who have carried out a large body of research into aggression,[1] particularly related to television and video games,[2] are clearly attracted to and respect his ideas.

On social learning theory specifically, they write, "It provides a useful set of concepts for understanding and describing the beliefs and expectations that guide social behavior. Social learning theory—especially key concepts regarding the development and change of expectations and how one construes the social world—is particularly useful in understanding the acquisition of aggressive behaviors and in explaining instrumental aggression."[3] They have expanded many of Bandura's ideas and are engaged in research into their further extension and use.

Additionally, in the course of his long career at Stanford University, Bandura has had contact with colleagues and students who are also now greatly respected in their various fields, many of whom have produced research into aggression, social learning theories, and self-regulation.* Education specialist Frank Pajares,* for example, spent much time investigating social cognitive theory and wrote biographies and websites about Bandura.[4]

Schools of Thought

Many other esteemed psychologists and academics have been associated with and are still developing Bandura's ideas of social cognitive theory and self-efficacy.* He could be seen as a founder of modern self-improvement literature. Bandura's ideas on self-regulation and self-efficacy, which first appeared in *Aggression*, have influenced one of the leaders in motivational theories, the psychologist Carol Dweck.* She has said that her theories about self-confidence and motivation draw on social cognitive theory, stating, "A simple belief about yourself … permeates every part of your life."[5] It is interesting to note that she also supervised the PhD of Mary Bandura (Albert's daughter).[6] Ideas about motivation are currently very popular research topics in a range of fields, from education to healthcare.

Researchers such as Craig Anderson have developed Bandura's ideas about aggression. Other theories of aggression have been proposed, but most of them closely resemble Bandura's cognitive theories.[7] Self-efficacy research,[8] founded on Bandura's concepts, now tends to focus on issues such as motivation and goal orientation. Self-determination theory[9] is concerned with how people motivate themselves and the choices they make.[10] These schools of thought have all had an influence on psychotherapy and how psychologists address behavioral problems.

In Current Scholarship

Albert Bandura continued to work on his theories of social cognitive theory, self-regulation, and self-efficacy after the publication of *Aggression: A Social Learning Analysis*. Today, psychologists tend to talk about his body of work as a whole rather than only discussing this book. One proponent of Bandura's ideas is Barry J. Zimmerman,* who has used Bandura's concepts of social cognitive theory and self-efficacy extensively in educational psychology,* or the study of psychological processes as they relate to institutional learning.

Zimmerman and his colleagues have investigated and developed questions of observational learning, self-regulation in academic learning, and self-efficacy. Zimmerman has added depth and detail to Bandura's concepts of social cognitive theory and self-regulation. He has developed, for example, the idea that self-efficacy in an academic setting is made up of three components: self-observation, self-judgment, and self-reaction. This concept is also linked to the study of behavior and aggressive tendencies among students.

Another advocate of Bandura's work is the late educator Frank Pajares, who wrote of Bandura, "Without him I would be lost at sea." He demonstrated his admiration by maintaining a website dedicated to Bandura and his work. In a candid interview, Pajares revealed, "My doctoral students and I spent two delightful days with [Bandura]. His work, as exemplified by his social cognitive theory of human functioning, serves as the theoretical foundation for my own efforts … Were it not for Professor Bandura's thinking and theorizing about the human condition, I would be much poorer intellectually and professionally."[11] This is exemplified in Pajares's work on self-efficacy, which he looked at in the context of educational psychology.

Bandura changed the perspective from which aggression was analyzed. His later development of social learning theory prompted a fundamental shift toward a cognitive perspective on human learning in the field of psychology. The conceptual framework that Bandura laid down forms the basis for a high proportion of psychology research today. His work has had a considerable impact on the direction of future research especially in the field of education, for which he was awarded the E. L. Thorndike Award in 1998.

NOTES

1   Craig A. Anderson and Brad J. Bushman, "Human Aggression," *Psychology* 53, no. 1 (2002): 27.

2   Craig A. Anderson, and Karen E. Dill, "Video Games and Aggressive Thoughts, Feelings, and Behavior in the Laboratory and in Life," *Journal of Personality and Social Psychology* 78, no. 4 (2000): 772.

3   Anderson and Bushman, "Human Aggression," 27–51.

4   M. Frank Pajares, "Albert Bandura: Biographical Sketch" (2004), http://www.uky.edu/~eushe2/Bandura/bandurabio.html.

5   Carol Dweck, *Mindset: The New Psychology of Success* (New York: Random House, 2006).

6   Marina Krakovsky, "The Effort Effect," *Stanford Magazine* March/April 2007, http://alumni.stanford.edu/get/page/magazine/article/?article_id=32124.

7   Anderson and Bushman, "Human Aggression."

8   Albert Bandura, Claudio Barbaranelli, Gian Vittorio Caprara, and Concetta Pastorelli, "Self-Efficacy Beliefs as Shapers of Children's Aspirations and Career Trajectories," *Child Development*, vol. 72, no.1 (2001): 187–206.

9   Idit Katz, and Bat-Hen Shahar, "What Makes a Motivating Teacher? Teachers' Motivation and Beliefs as Predictors of Their Autonomy-supportive Style," *School Psychology International* 36, no. 6 (2015): 575–88.

10 Edward L. Deci and Richard M. Ryan, *Intrinsic Motivation and Self-determination in Human Behavior* (New York: Springer Science & Business Media, 1985).

11 Héfer Bembenutty, "The Last Word, An Interview with Frank Pajares: God, the Devil, William James, the Little Prince, and Self-Efficacy," *Journal of Advanced Academics* 18, no. 4 (2007): 665.

MODULE 11
IMPACT AND INFLUENCE TODAY

KEY POINTS

- *Aggression* is one of the most important scholarly texts in the history of psychology.

- When people talk about violence in the media, they most frequently cite Bandura, particularly his Bobo doll experiments.*

- Bandura has also turned his attention to themes such as terrorism and institutional violence.

Position

The ideas that Albert Bandura develops in *Aggression: A Social Learning Analysis* (1973) are still of great interest and relevance today. "Since World War II," it has been noted, "homicide rates have actually increased rather than decreased in a number of industrialized countries, most notably the United States. Thus, in recent years there has been renewed interest in learning why humans sometimes behave aggressively."[1] This is particularly pertinent to the rapid development and popularity of the Internet, social media, and video games.[2] Not only are children and adults exposed to relatively uncensored images and information but also news of aggressive acts can be communicated and promoted rapidly.

The persistence of aggression in modern developed society demonstrates the need to consider it, just as Bandura did, both from a theoretical point of view and in terms of the practical steps that might reduce it. It should be noted, however, that not everyone shares the perception that violence is increasing in modern society. Steven Pinker,* an influential Canadian psychologist and linguist, argues the

> **❝** Seen from the sociocognitive* perspective, human nature is a vast potentiality that can be fashioned by direct and observational experience into a variety of forms within biological limits. **❞**
>
> Bryant Jennings and Mary Beth Oliver, *Media effects: Advances in theory and research*

opposite in *The Better Angels of Our Nature: Why Violence has Declined.*[3] While Pinker's view might not make it any less necessary to study aggression, if he is right, that might change the direction and methods of research into aggression.

There has been an increase in research focusing on positive outcomes rather than the negative aspects of human behavior and on concepts such as self-regulation* and self-efficacy* (the capacity to control one's own behavior, and one's belief in that capacity) that Bandura coined in his text.[4] The ideas that Bandura put forward in *Aggression* are still relevant today and have transformed the field of psychology by bridging behaviorism* and cognitive psychology.*

Interaction

An extensive search of books and articles shows that many contemporary thinkers accept Bandura's ideas (in part or as a whole) and employ them in a great many fields. There are no serious criticisms among psychologists of his theories concerning social cognitive theory* or social learning theory* and self-efficacy. With regards to aggression, American psychologist Craig Anderson* said in a 2002 review, "Social learning theory—especially key concepts regarding the development and change of expectations and how one construes the social world—is particularly useful in understanding the acquisition of aggressive behaviors and in explaining instrumental aggression."[5]

Indeed, many other theories of aggression that have developed since the publication of *Aggression* are versions of Bandura's original social learning theory. One of the main goals in contemporary aggression studies is to understand cognitive processes and to offer practical strategies for behavior change. In this sense, Bandura's theories are more than just academic; they are also relevant in practically treating behavioral issues.

Current researchers in the field of aggression face similar challenges to those that Bandura faced. For example, he was concerned with the media's influence on children's development. While this remains an important area of study today, the accelerated change that social media and new communications technology has brought about is likely to make it even harder to analyze the complex web of links between media representations and social behavior.

The Continuing Debate

The newest developments in the study of aggression have come from advances in genetics and neuroscience* (the science of the brain and the nervous system). Some researchers have argued that aggressiveness may be in fact a biological trait,* defined as "an enduring disposition toward physical assault,"[6] and important in models that predict which young people will go on to be violent later in life. Recent research has suggested that neurochemical* correlates, or specific aspects of brain chemistry, can be observed in those who are seen as displaying the trait of aggressiveness.

Although the studies are in their infancy, there is evidence that monoamine oxidase (MAO-A),* an enzyme involved in metabolizing chemicals in the brain, may behave unusually in the bodies of those who display aggressive behavior. Importantly, MAO-A is involved in the release and inhibition of the neurochemicals dopamine,* serotonin,* and norepinephrine,* which are associated with the regulation of emotion. It also appears that there are gene–environment interactions, as the researchers explain: "Low MAO-A genotype was associated with antisocial behavior and high self-reported trait aggression only with childhood exposure to severe maltreatment, thus highlighting the significance of the interplay between genes and environment."[7]

Thus, while this new research may appear biological in nature, it is highlighting that environmental and social factors are still extremely important. In this sense, it could still be seen as a continuation of Bandura's early work on aggression.

NOTES

1   Craig A. Anderson and Brad J. Bushman, "Human Aggression," *Psychology* 53, no. 1 (2002): 28.

2   Craig A. Anderson and Karen E. Dill, "Video Games and Aggressive Thoughts, Feelings, and Behavior in the Laboratory and in Life," 772–90.

3   Steven Pinker, *The Better Angels of Our Nature: Why Violence has Declined* (New York: Viking, 2011).

4   Karen D. Multon, Steven D. Brown and Robert W. Lent, "Relation of Self-Efficacy Beliefs to Academic Outcomes: A Meta-Analytic Investigation," *Journal of Counseling Psychology* 38, no. 1 (1991), 30–8.

5   Anderson and Bushman, "Human Aggression," 31.

6   Nelly Alia-Klein et al, "Brain Monoamine Oxidase-A Activity Predicts Trait Aggression," *The Journal of Neuroscience* 28, no. 19 (2008): 5099–104.

7   Alia-Klein, et al, "Brain," 5104.

WHERE NEXT?

KEY POINTS

- Bandura's *Aggression* is likely to continue to be the seminal social psychological explanation for why humans behave aggressively.

- As a key social psychology text, the book is likely to continue to influence policies and academic thought.

- *Aggression* is highly influential due to its groundbreaking approach, using experiments rather than psychoanalytic* theories, and its broad readership.

Potential

Aggression: a Social Learning Analysis by Albert Bandura deserves special attention because the author outlines ideas in it that still dominate thinking about human behavior in psychology and other fields more than 40 years after the book's publication. His work remains relevant across many questions of academic and social interest, such as how schoolchildren learn and how the media affects society.

Although Bandura developed his ideas on aggression in the context of social learning theory after the publication of *Aggression*, his key points still hold true in his work as a whole and are as pertinent today as when they were written in the 1970s. His work on imitation,* the development of laboratory-based methods, experimental social psychology, vicarious modeling* and factors that control and maintain aggression are now embedded in the accepted canon of psychology and social sciences, and even in everyday popular debate.

Social learning* or social cognitive theory* continues to have a vast impact across many fields, such as criminology and sociology, not

> **❝ You have made 'Bobo' a doll for all times. ❞**
> Frank Pajares, *APA Conference, Hawaii,* 2004

only as a conceptual framework for academic activity but also in practical areas, such as prisons, education, and healthcare. Bandura's conceptual frameworks are used by scholars in areas of psychology ranging from educational to counseling.

For example, the scholar Joan E. Grusec* outlines Bandura's importance to developmental psychology (how we develop psychologically from infancy), C. Ray Jeffery* uses Bandura's thought in the context of criminology, and Barry J. Zimmerman has used the same theories in the field of educational psychology. Bandura's social learning theory has shaped government policy on issues such as the media, education, and healthcare in many different countries.

Future Directions

The book still forms the conceptual basis for many academic studies and practical attempts to control and modify behavior. Bandura is currently concentrating on this element of his research and has had particular success with the use of social cognitive theory in the prevention of HIV, the virus that causes the disease AIDS.[1] Bandura explains that "both self regulative and risk reduction strategies for dealing with a variety of situations that promote risky behavior should be modeled to convey general guides that can be applied and adjusted to fit changing circumstances."[2] In other words, Bandura's ideas about how individuals think about themselves and how they learn and maintain behaviors can be used to help improve sexual health in populations by reducing risky behavior. As this example suggests, social cognitive theory is applicable to many important societal issues.

The continuing debate about the influence of depictions of violence in the media on aggression in society shows no signs of slowing down. Recent breakthroughs in genetics and neuroscience are highlighting the relationship between biology and environment, showing that brain chemicals change in response to an individual's life experiences and conditions. Particularly in the field of aggression, it seems that understanding learning processes like modeling, imitation, and observation and how they interact with biological processes will become ever more important. Future research in the field of biology will no doubt look at MAO-A,* an enzyme associated with aggressive behavior, and the role of neurochemistry* in human behavior. This new field that is looking at the interaction of all of these aspects is called epigenetics.*

Summary

Bandura has provided a large body of work that has inspired doctoral students and others in various fields. His work has been crucial to many people. For example, the educator Frank Pajares writes, "His work, as exemplified by his social cognitive theory of human functioning, serves as the theoretical foundation for my own efforts … Professor Bandura charts the waters I navigate."[3]

Before Bandura, nobody had brought together the ideas of social learning and aggression in such great detail. He applied the relatively new and underdeveloped concept of social learning to aggression and produced the first truly coherent account of the theory. He delivered that advice to a broad audience in *Aggression*, which also contained practical advice that resonated beyond the academic world. Bandura made a scholarly subject accessible to the educated layperson while maintaining academic rigor, as one reviewer remarks, "This book is evidence of both the scholarly strength and value commitments of its author."[4]

Finally, Bandura presented a number of his laboratory-based studies, which were relatively novel and cleverly designed for the time. As Joan E. Grusec says of Bandura's "very clever use of laboratory analogs of real-life situations" to test his theories, "The ability to manipulate independent variables in controlled settings and to draw causal conclusions provided a solution for one of the great problems of the correlational approach of [Robert] Sears,* and it appeared to be another giant step forward in making the study of social development a truly scientific undertaking."[5]

NOTES

1   Albert Bandura, "Social Cognitive Theory and Exercise of Control over HIV Infection," in *Preventing AIDS: Theories and Methods of Behavioral Interventions*, eds. Ralph J. DiClemente and John L. Peterson (New York: Springer, 1994), 25–59.

2   Bandura, "Social Cognitive Theory," 37.

3   Héfer Bembenutty, "The Last Word, An Interview with Frank Pajares: God, the Devil, William James, the Little Prince, and Self-Efficacy," *Journal of Advanced Academics* 18, No.4 (2007), 665.

4   Alan C. Kerckhoff, "Review of *Aggression: A Social Learning Analysis* by Albert Bandura," *American Journal of Sociology 80*, no.1 (1974), 250.

5   Joan E. Grusec, "Social Learning Theory and Developmental Psychology: The Legacies of Robert Sears and Albert Bandura," Developmental Psychology 28, no.5 (1992), 784.

GLOSSARY

GLOSSARY OF TERMS

Agentic: the concept that while humans respond to stimuli in the environment, they are also cognitive agents (capable of autonomous thought) and are able to produce an effect on the society around them. "Agentic" denotes a person's capacity to influence their reality rather than the other way around.

American Psychological Association (APA): the largest professional organization that represents the various fields of psychology in the United States.

Aurora Shootings: an incident in 2012 when a young man walked into a movie theater during a screening in Aurora, Colorado, and committed a mass shooting.

Behaviorism: a school of thought arguing that human action can be viewed as a process of responses to any given stimulus.

Beta: in animal species, the beta is of a lower social order than the pack leaders, who are known as alphas.

Bobo doll experiments: experiments that Albert Bandura and his colleagues undertook that showed that when children observed violence they were more likely to behave violently.

Brain imaging: the practice of observing the brain by using equipment such as functional resonance imaging.

Catharsis: an act of emotional renewal or release.

Civil Rights Movement: a number of mostly nonviolent political organizations engaged in the struggle of civil and political equality for minority groups in the United States. During the 1950s and 1960s, this movement was aimed at abolishing racial discrimination and improving the civil rights of African Americans.

Cognition: the working processes of the brain that enable us to learn about and understand our environment. For example, we process information that we receive from our senses and our environment *cognitively*.

Cognitive Neoassociation: the theory that we will behave in a certain manner due to attributions from a previous experience—that is, we may label an emotion as anger if a similar situation that we previously encountered produced anger.

Cognitive psychology: the school of psychology concerned with how cognition affects behavior.

Cold War: a prolonged state of political and military tension between the Soviet Union and powerful Western countries led by the United States. The Cold War is often dated 1947–1991 and featured cycles of relative calm and rising tensions. The war was so named because the United States and Soviet Union never met in direct military combat, although each possessed nuclear weapons that threatened the other.

Collective aggression: a situation that occurs when a number of people behave aggressively together.

Columbine Massacre: a 1999 mass shooting at Columbine High School, Colorado, committed by two of its students.

Counseling psychology: the practice of using psychological theory in order to help patients through emotional problems.

Darwinian: relating to the theories of the founding evolutionary biologist Charles Darwin.

Determinates: the factors that predict an outcome.

Drive theories: theories stating that specific unconscious impulses lead people to behave in particular ways.

Ecological validity: the extent to which findings from experiments and laboratory research can be applied to real-world conditions.

Empirical evidence: evidence that is founded upon experiment and observation.

Eros: in Freudian theory, a drive that subconsciously pushes us to cling on to life.

Ethological: behavior with evolutionary roots, intended to facilitate survival and reproduction.

Experimental psychology: the practice of psychological research conducted with empirical experiments.

Evidence-based practice: the use of the results of (mostly) quantitative studies (studies that produce measurable, numerical information) to inform clinical protocol.

Evolutionary: associated with the process of evolution.

Freudian: related to the ideas of the psychoanalyst Sigmund Freud.

Frustration–aggression hypothesis: an idea suggesting that aggression arises due to the interruption of a specific goal, which causes frustration.

Genome mapping: the practice of recording sequences of genes (mostly conducted to investigate which genes are responsible for illness).

Imitation: the act of copying.

Instinctual Theory: the theory that behavior is driven by evolutionary instinct (that is, genetically programmed desires to survive and reproduce).

Locus of control: the amount of control an individual believes they can exert over their environment.

Milgram Experiments: experiments carried out by Stanley Milgram that involved investigating how far authority figures could push people to commit harmful acts.

Monoamine Oxidase (MAO-A): an enzyme involved in metabolizing chemicals in the brain.

Modeling: using the actions of another person as an example of how to form new behaviors.

Naturalistic behavior: behavior that occurs in everyday life (that is, not manipulated in a laboratory or in an experiment).

Neoassociation: a term from Behaviorist theory that describes behavior associated with conditioned or unconditioned responses

Neuroscience: the science of the brain and the nervous system, sometimes used interchangeably with the term "neurobiology." Neuroscience looks at how the nervous system works and malfunctions—and can be manipulated.

Neurochemical: chemicals in the brain, such as neurotransmitters responsible for normal (and sometimes abnormal) functioning.

Neurotransmitter: chemicals in the brain that allow brain cells (neurons) to communicate.

Norepinephrine: a neurotransmitter involved in stress reactions.

Observation: learning though watching another individual.

Operant conditioning: a description of the learning process as through reinforcement or punishment.

Performance catharsis: the idea that performing an act will release the pressure of struggling *not* to perform that act.

Primary response: in Freudian theory, a behavior that arises as a result of other drives being suppressed—mainly the drive to seek pleasure or avoid pain.

Psychoanalytic: a school of thought founded by Sigmund Freud that seeks to explain and treat behavior by understanding unconscious drives and disruptions in early development.

Psychologist: a person who works in the field of understanding human thought, action, and behavior.

Quantitative: describes data that is measurable in real terms such as reaction time or height.

Reciprocal determination: a theory that not only does our environment—our families, peers and the media—affect our behavior, but also that our cognition has an effect on our environment.

Regulatory function: a mechanism that helps to reproduce and maintain certain habits in an individual or society.

Reinforcement: a consequence of an action likely to promote repetition of that behavior in the future through association—for example, a reward given to a dog for adequately performing a task.

Scientific method: a general term describing a range of objective techniques that scientists use to measure quantifiable data or explain phenomena.

Self-regulation: the ability to control your own behavior.

Serotonin: a type of neurotransmitter.

Self-efficacy: a term that Bandura defined as "the belief in one's capabilities to organize and execute the courses of action required to manage prospective situations."

Sociocognitive: the integration of social and cognitive theory. This theory describes how our social world provides the learning environment by which we cognitively learn how to behave.

Social cognitive theory: an alternative name given to social learning theory that Bandura coined to aid clarity. It may be considered a framework for describing the interrelations of environment, cognition (thinking and understanding), and behavior— founded on the core assumptions that behavior is learned through observation, imitation, and modeling.

Social learning theory: the theory that behavior occurs due to learning though the social processes of observation, imitation and modeling.

Social psychologist: a psychologist who is interested in how social factors shape the behavior of a population or person.

Socialization: the process by which we learn to interact with our social environment.

Survival of the fittest: the Darwinian precept that traits evolve in species in order to facilitate survival (or that they offer the prospect of survival when environmental changes cause other competing organisms to die out); surviving organisms therefore pass on these beneficial genes.

Thanatos: a Freudian drive that subconsciously pushes us to destroy ourselves.

Trait: a genetic aspect of an individual.

Unconscious: in Freudian theory, the part of the mind that cannot be perfectly or easily known, but nevertheless informs behavior. The term can also refer to physical processes that can be accomplished without deliberate thought, such as walking.

Vicarious learning: learning though the observation of the actions of others and from the environment at large.

Vietnam War: a conflict that occurred between 1955 and 1975 in Vietnam, Laos, and Cambodia. North Vietnam, supported by China and its communist allies, fought the government of South Vietnam, which the United States and other anti-communist allies supported. American involvement in the conflict started in the 1950s and escalated in the early 1960s. Combat units began to be deployed in 1965. The escalation of American involvement in the war was highly controversial and sparked nationwide antiwar protests in the United States.

World War II: a global conflict that took place between 1939 and 1945. It started as a European conflict between Germany and her neighbors, which resulted in the eruption of tensions around the world. The United States entered the conflict in 1941. The war ended with the defeat of Germany and her allies and the dropping of atomic bombs on Hiroshima and Nagasaki in Japan. About 50 million people died before the war was brought to an end.

Zimbardo Prison Experiments: a 1971 experiment by Stanford University psychologist Philip Zimbardo, set in a prison-like laboratory. The experiment split half the subjects into prison guards and the other into prison inmates. Zimbardo wanted to examine whether taking on these roles would change the participants' behavior.

PEOPLE MENTIONED IN THE TEXT

Craig A. Anderson (b. 1955) is an American psychologist. He is director of the Center for the Study of Violence at Iowa State University. His research interests in aggression include the study of the effects of violent video games on children.

Leonard Berkowitz (b. 1926) is a professor of social psychology at the University of Wisconsin at Madison. He is best known for originating the cognitive neoassociation model of aggressive behavior, which suggests that previous experiences influence our behavior.

Brad J. Bushman (b. 1961) is a professor of communication and psychology at Ohio State University. His research interests include the causes, consequences, and solutions to the problem of human aggression and violence.

John Dollard (1900–80) was an American psychologist and social scientist, well known for his work on frustration-related aggression.

Carol S. Dweck (b. 1946) is a professor of psychology at Stanford University known for her research into the mindsets (self-conceptions) that influence people's motivations and how they behave.

Charles Darwin (1809–82) is considered the founder of evolutionary theory, having laid out his theories on evolution in his seminal work, *On the Origins of Species* (1859). Darwin realized that animal traits evolved as a result of being advantageous to survival.

Sigmund Freud (1856–1939) was an eminent Austrian psychologist and neurologist who became famous for his psychoanalytical theories, commonly used in the therapeutic process of psychoanalysis. His best known works include *The Interpretation of Dreams* (1900) and *Five Lectures on Psycho-Analysis* (1916).

Joan E. Grusec (b. 1978) studies how different parenting styles effect children emotionally and socially. She currently has a lab at Stanford University.

David Starr Jordan (1851–1931) was the founder of Stanford University.

Konrad Lorenz (1903–89) was an Austrian-born scholar who received a Nobel prize in 1973. He is widely considered one of the founders of modern ethological study (the study of human behavior).

Mark A. May was an American psychologist. He was director of the Institute of Human Relations at Yale University between 1935 and 1960.

Neal Elgar Miller (1909–2002) was an American psychologist whose works included studies into biofeedback (the way that the organism becomes aware of its own processes) and behavioral theories.

Frank Pajares was a professor of educational psychology at Emory University, who studied self-efficacy in academic settings and academic motivation. His scholarship also focused on the life of William James, the psychologist and philosopher. Pajares died in 2009.

Steven Pinker (b. 1954) is a professor of psychology at Harvard University who specializes in evolutionary and cognitive psychology—particularly the acquisition of language and visual cognition.

C. Ray Jeffrey (1921–2007) was president of the American Society of Criminology and Professor of Criminology at Florida State University. Notable for his multidisciplinary approach, he came to prominence after the publication of his book *Crime Prevention through Environmental Design* (1977).

Julian Rotter (b. 1916) is an American psychologist famous for social learning theories.

Robert Sears (1908–89) was head of the psychology department at Stanford University and received the American Psychological Association's Distinguished Scientific Contribution Award in 1975. He worked in various fields but specialized in child development.

Burrhus Frederic Skinner (1904–90) was an American psychologist noted for his contributions to behaviorist theory. He is most famous for describing operant conditioning, which concerns how learning occurs through reinforcement of a given behavior.

Barry J. Zimmerman is a professor of educational psychology at the City University of New York City. The recipient of the E. L. Thorndike award in 1999, he has published extensively on theories of self-regulated learning and motivation.

WORKS CITED

WORKS CITED

APA Conference, Hawaii, July/August 2004, http://www.uky.edu/~eushe2/Bandura/BanduraAPA2004.html.

Alia-Klein, Nelly, Rita Z. Goldstein, Aarti Kriplani, Jean Logan, Dardo Tomasi, Benjamin Williams, Frank Telang et al. "Brain Monoamine Oxidase A Activity Predicts Trait Aggression." *The Journal of Neuroscience* 28, no. 19 (2008): 5099–104.

Anderson, Craig A. and Karen E. Dill. "Video Games and Aggressive Thoughts, Feelings, and Behavior in the Laboratory and in Life," *Journal of Personality and Social Psychology* 78, no. 4 (2000): 772–90.

Anderson, Craig A. and Brad J. Bushman. "Human Aggression." *Psychology* 53, no. 1 (2002): 27–51

Bandura, Albert. "Autobiography." In *A History of Psychology in Autobiography*, vol. 9, edited by M. G. Lindzey and W. M. Runyan. Washington DC: American Psychological Association, 2007.

Aggression: A Social Learning Analysis, Prentice-Hall Series in Social Learning Theory. New Jersey: Prentice-Hall Englewood Cliffs, 1973.

"Mechanisms of Moral Disengagement in Terrorism." *Origins of Terrorism: Psychologies, Ideologies, States of Mind* (1990): 161–91.

Self Efficacy: The Exercise of Control. New York: W. H. Freeman and Company, 1997.

"Social Cognitive Theory of Self-regulation." *Organizational Behavior and Human Decision Processes* 50, no. 2 (1991): 248–87.

"Self-efficacy: Toward a Unifying Theory of Behavioral Change." *Psychological Review* 84, no. 2 (1977): 191–215

"Social Cognitive Theory and Exercise of Control over HIV Infection." In *Preventing AIDS*. New York: Springe, 1994.

Bandura, Albert, and Forest J. Jourden. "Self-regulatory Mechanisms Governing the Impact of Social Comparison on Complex Decision Making." *Journal of Personality and Social Psychology* 60, no. 6 (1991): 941.

Bandura, Albert and Richard H. Walters. *Adolescent Aggression: A Study of the Influence of Child-Training practices and Family Interrelationships.* New York: Ronald Press,1959.

Bembenutty, Héfer. "The Last Word: An Interview with Frank Pajares: God, the Devil, William James, the Little Prince, and Self-Efficacy." *Journal of Advanced Academics* 18, no. 4 (2007): 660–77.

Berkowitz, Leonard. "Frustration-Aggression Hypothesis: Examination and Reformulation." *Psychological Bulletin* 106, no. 1 (1989): 59.

Bjørkly, Stål. "Psychological Theories of Aggression: Principles and Application to Practice." In *Violence in Mental Health Settings*, edited by Dirk Richter and Richard Whittington. New York: Springer, 2006.

Bronfenbrenner, Urie. "Toward an Experimental Ecology of Human Development." *American Psychologist* 32, no. 7 (1977): 513–31.

Campbell, James M. "Book Reviews: No Peace in Our Time? Review of *Aggression: A Social Learning Analysis* by Albert Bandura." *Criminal Justice and Behavior* 2, no. 91 (1975): 91–3.

Coates, Brian and Willard W. Hartup. "Age and Verbalization in Observational Learning." *Developmental Psychology* 1, no. 5 (1969), 556–62.

Deci, Edward L., and Richard M. Ryan. *Intrinsic Motivation and Self-Determination in Human Behavior*. New York: Springer Science & Business Media, 1985.

Dollard, John, Neal E. Miller, Leonard W. Doob, Orval Hobart Mowrer, and Robert R. Sears. *Frustration and Aggression*. New Haven, CT: Yale University Press, 1939.

Dweck, Carol. *Mindset: The New Psychology of Success*. New York: Random House, 2006.

Ferguson, Christopher, J. *Adolescents, Crime, and the Media: A Critical Analysis*. New York: Springer, 2013.

Feshbach, Seymour and Robert D. Singer. *Television and Aggression: An Experimental Field Study.* San Francisco: Jossey-Bass, 1971.

Foster, Christine. "Confidence Man." *Stanford Magazine*, September/October 2006. http://alumni.stanford.edu/get/page/magazine/article/?article_id=33332.

Grusec, Joan E. "Social Learning Theory and Developmental Psychology: The legacies of Robert Sears and Albert Bandura." *Developmental Psychology* 28, no. 5 (1992): 776.

Hart, Karen E., F. Scholar, W. A. Kristonis, and D. Alumnus. "Critical Analysis of an Original Writing on Social Learning Theory: Imitation of Film-mediated Aggressive Models By: Albert Bandura, Dorothea Ross and Sheila A. Ross." In *National Forum of Applied Educational Research Journal*, 20, no. 3. (2006): 1–7.

Jeffery, C. Ray. "Criminology as an Interdisciplinary Behavioral Science." *Criminology* 16, no. 2 (1978): 149–69.

Jennings Bryant, and Mary Beth Oliver, eds. *Media effects: Advances in Theory and Research*. New York: Routledge, 2009.

Kerckhoff, Alan C. "Review of *Aggression: A Social Learning Analysis*, by Albert Bandura." *American Journal of Sociology* 80, no. 1 (1974): 250–1.

Krakovsky, Marina. "The Effort Effect." *Stanford Magazine* March/April 2007. https://alumni.stanford.edu/get/page/magazine/article/?article_id=32124.

Lansford, Jennifer E. "Beyond Bandura's Bobo Doll Studies." In *Developmental Psychology: Revisiting the Classic Studies*. Edited by Alan M. Slater and Paul C. Quinn. London: SAGE, 2012.

Lindenfors, Patrik, and Tullberg, Birgitta S. "Evolutionary Aspects of Aggression: The Importance of Sexual Selection." *Advances in Genetics* 75 (2011): 7.

Lorenz, Konrad. *On Aggression*. New York/London: Routledge, 2002.

Miller, Neal Elgar, and John Dollard. *Social Learning and Imitation*. New Haven: Yale University Press.

Multon, Karen D., Steven D. Brown, and Robert W. Lent. "Relation of Self-Efficacy Beliefs to Academic Outcomes: A Meta-Analytic Investigation." *Journal of Counseling Psychology* 38, no. 1 (1991): 30–8.

Pajares, M. Frank. *Albert Bandura: Biographical sketch*. 2004. http://des.emory.edu/mfp/bandurabio.html.

Pinker, Steven. *The Better Angels of Our Nature: Why Violence has Declined*. New York: Viking, 2011.

Rotter, Julian B. *The Development and Applications of Social Learning Theory: Selected Papers*. Connecticut: Praeger Publishers, 1982.

Skinner, Burphus Frederic, and C. B. Ferster. *Schedules of Reinforcement*. B. F. Skinner Foundation, 2015.

Touhey, John C. "Review of *Aggression: A Social Learning Analysis* by Albert Bandura." *Contemporary Sociology* 4, no. 2 (1975): 169–71.

Wels, Susan, "The Troubles at Stanford: Student Uprisings in the 1960s and '70s." *Sandstone and Tile* 35, no. 1 (2011).

Zimmerman Barry J. and Dale H. Schunk. "Albert Bandura: The Man and His Contributions to Educational Psychology." In *Educational Psychology: One-Hundred Years of Contributions*. New Jersey: Lawrence Earlbaum, 2003.

THE MACAT LIBRARY
BY DISCIPLINE

AFRICANA STUDIES

Chinua Achebe's *An Image of Africa: Racism in Conrad's Heart of Darkness*
W. E. B. Du Bois's *The Souls of Black Folk*
Zora Neale Huston's *Characteristics of Negro Expression*
Martin Luther King Jr's *Why We Can't Wait*
Toni Morrison's *Playing in the Dark: Whiteness in the American Literary Imagination*

ANTHROPOLOGY

Arjun Appadurai's *Modernity at Large: Cultural Dimensions of Globalisation*
Philippe Ariès's *Centuries of Childhood*
Franz Boas's *Race, Language and Culture*
Kim Chan & Renée Mauborgne's *Blue Ocean Strategy*
Jared Diamond's *Guns, Germs & Steel: the Fate of Human Societies*
Jared Diamond's *Collapse: How Societies Choose to Fail or Survive*
E. E. Evans-Pritchard's *Witchcraft, Oracles and Magic Among the Azande*
James Ferguson's *The Anti-Politics Machine*
Clifford Geertz's *The Interpretation of Cultures*
David Graeber's *Debt: the First 5000 Years*
Karen Ho's *Liquidated: An Ethnography of Wall Street*
Geert Hofstede's *Culture's Consequences: Comparing Values, Behaviors, Institutes and Organizations across Nations*
Claude Lévi-Strauss's *Structural Anthropology*
Jay Macleod's *Ain't No Makin' It: Aspirations and Attainment in a Low-Income Neighborhood*
Saba Mahmood's *The Politics of Piety: The Islamic Revival and the Feminist Subjec*t
Marcel Mauss's *The Gift*

BUSINESS

Jean Lave & Etienne Wenger's *Situated Learning*
Theodore Levitt's *Marketing Myopia*
Burton G. Malkiel's *A Random Walk Down Wall Street*
Douglas McGregor's *The Human Side of Enterprise*
Michael Porter's *Competitive Strategy: Creating and Sustaining Superior Performance*
John Kotter's *Leading Change*
C. K. Prahalad & Gary Hamel's *The Core Competence of the Corporation*

CRIMINOLOGY

Michelle Alexander's *The New Jim Crow: Mass Incarceration in the Age of Colorblindness*
Michael R. Gottfredson & Travis Hirschi's *A General Theory of Crime*
Richard Herrnstein & Charles A. Murray's *The Bell Curve: Intelligence and Class Structure in American Life*
Elizabeth Loftus's *Eyewitness Testimony*
Jay Macleod's *Ain't No Makin' It: Aspirations and Attainment in a Low-Income Neighborhood*
Philip Zimbardo's *The Lucifer Effect*

ECONOMICS

Janet Abu-Lughod's *Before European Hegemony*
Ha-Joon Chang's *Kicking Away the Ladder*
David Brion Davis's *The Problem of Slavery in the Age of Revolution*
Milton Friedman's *The Role of Monetary Policy*
Milton Friedman's *Capitalism and Freedom*
David Graeber's *Debt: the First 5000 Years*
Friedrich Hayek's *The Road to Serfdom*
Karen Ho's *Liquidated: An Ethnography of Wall Street*

The Macat Library By Discipline

John Maynard Keynes's *The General Theory of Employment, Interest and Money*
Charles P. Kindleberger's *Manias, Panics and Crashes*
Robert Lucas's *Why Doesn't Capital Flow from Rich to Poor Countries?*
Burton G. Malkiel's *A Random Walk Down Wall Street*
Thomas Robert Malthus's *An Essay on the Principle of Population*
Karl Marx's *Capital*
Thomas Piketty's *Capital in the Twenty-First Century*
Amartya Sen's *Development as Freedom*
Adam Smith's *The Wealth of Nations*
Nassim Nicholas Taleb's *The Black Swan: The Impact of the Highly Improbable*
Amos Tversky's & Daniel Kahneman's *Judgment under Uncertainty: Heuristics and Biases*
Mahbub Ul Haq's *Reflections on Human Development*
Max Weber's *The Protestant Ethic and the Spirit of Capitalism*

FEMINISM AND GENDER STUDIES

Judith Butler's *Gender Trouble*
Simone De Beauvoir's *The Second Sex*
Michel Foucault's *History of Sexuality*
Betty Friedan's *The Feminine Mystique*
Saba Mahmood's *The Politics of Piety: The Islamic Revival and the Feminist Subject*
Joan Wallach Scott's *Gender and the Politics of History*
Mary Wollstonecraft's *A Vindication of the Rights of Woman*
Virginia Woolf's *A Room of One's Own*

GEOGRAPHY

The Brundtland Report's *Our Common Future*
Rachel Carson's *Silent Spring*
Charles Darwin's *On the Origin of Species*
James Ferguson's *The Anti-Politics Machine*
Jane Jacobs's *The Death and Life of Great American Cities*
James Lovelock's *Gaia: A New Look at Life on Earth*
Amartya Sen's *Development as Freedom*
Mathis Wackernagel & William Rees's *Our Ecological Footprint*

HISTORY

Janet Abu-Lughod's *Before European Hegemony*
Benedict Anderson's *Imagined Communities*
Bernard Bailyn's *The Ideological Origins of the American Revolution*
Hanna Batatu's *The Old Social Classes And The Revolutionary Movements Of Iraq*
Christopher Browning's *Ordinary Men: Reserve Police Batallion 101 and the Final Solution in Poland*
Edmund Burke's *Reflections on the Revolution in France*
William Cronon's *Nature's Metropolis: Chicago And The Great West*
Alfred W. Crosby's *The Columbian Exchange*
Hamid Dabashi's *Iran: A People Interrupted*
David Brion Davis's *The Problem of Slavery in the Age of Revolution*
Nathalie Zemon Davis's *The Return of Martin Guerre*
Jared Diamond's *Guns, Germs & Steel: the Fate of Human Societies*
Frank Dikotter's *Mao's Great Famine*
John W Dower's *War Without Mercy: Race And Power In The Pacific War*
W. E. B. Du Bois's *The Souls of Black Folk*
Richard J. Evans's *In Defence of History*
Lucien Febvre's *The Problem of Unbelief in the 16th Century*
Sheila Fitzpatrick's *Everyday Stalinism*

Eric Foner's *Reconstruction: America's Unfinished Revolution, 1863-1877*
Michel Foucault's *Discipline and Punish*
Michel Foucault's *History of Sexuality*
Francis Fukuyama's *The End of History and the Last Man*
John Lewis Gaddis's *We Now Know: Rethinking Cold War History*
Ernest Gellner's *Nations and Nationalism*
Eugene Genovese's *Roll, Jordan, Roll: The World the Slaves Made*
Carlo Ginzburg's *The Night Battles*
Daniel Goldhagen's *Hitler's Willing Executioners*
Jack Goldstone's *Revolution and Rebellion in the Early Modern World*
Antonio Gramsci's *The Prison Notebooks*
Alexander Hamilton, John Jay & James Madison's *The Federalist Papers*
Christopher Hill's *The World Turned Upside Down*
Carole Hillenbrand's *The Crusades: Islamic Perspectives*
Thomas Hobbes's *Leviathan*
Eric Hobsbawm's *The Age Of Revolution*
John A. Hobson's *Imperialism: A Study*
Albert Hourani's *History of the Arab Peoples*
Samuel P. Huntington's *The Clash of Civilizations and the Remaking of World Order*
C. L. R. James's *The Black Jacobins*
Tony Judt's *Postwar: A History of Europe Since 1945*
Ernst Kantorowicz's *The King's Two Bodies: A Study in Medieval Political Theology*
Paul Kennedy's *The Rise and Fall of the Great Powers*
Ian Kershaw's *The "Hitler Myth": Image and Reality in the Third Reich*
John Maynard Keynes's *The General Theory of Employment, Interest and Money*
Charles P. Kindleberger's *Manias, Panics and Crashes*
Martin Luther King Jr's *Why We Can't Wait*
Henry Kissinger's *World Order: Reflections on the Character of Nations and the Course of History*
Thomas Kuhn's *The Structure of Scientific Revolutions*
Georges Lefebvre's *The Coming of the French Revolution*
John Locke's *Two Treatises of Government*
Niccolò Machiavelli's *The Prince*
Thomas Robert Malthus's *An Essay on the Principle of Population*
Mahmood Mamdani's *Citizen and Subject: Contemporary Africa And The Legacy Of Late Colonialism*
Karl Marx's *Capital*
Stanley Milgram's *Obedience to Authority*
John Stuart Mill's *On Liberty*
Thomas Paine's *Common Sense*
Thomas Paine's *Rights of Man*
Geoffrey Parker's *Global Crisis: War, Climate Change and Catastrophe in the Seventeenth Century*
Jonathan Riley-Smith's *The First Crusade and the Idea of Crusading*
Jean-Jacques Rousseau's *The Social Contract*
Joan Wallach Scott's *Gender and the Politics of History*
Theda Skocpol's *States and Social Revolutions*
Adam Smith's *The Wealth of Nations*
Timothy Snyder's *Bloodlands: Europe Between Hitler and Stalin*
Sun Tzu's *The Art of War*
Keith Thomas's *Religion and the Decline of Magic*
Thucydides's *The History of the Peloponnesian War*
Frederick Jackson Turner's *The Significance of the Frontier in American History*
Odd Arne Westad's *The Global Cold War: Third World Interventions And The Making Of Our Times*

The Macat Library By Discipline

LITERATURE

Chinua Achebe's *An Image of Africa: Racism in Conrad's Heart of Darkness*
Roland Barthes's *Mythologies*
Homi K. Bhabha's *The Location of Culture*
Judith Butler's *Gender Trouble*
Simone De Beauvoir's *The Second Sex*
Ferdinand De Saussure's *Course in General Linguistics*
T. S. Eliot's *The Sacred Wood: Essays on Poetry and Criticism*
Zora Neale Huston's *Characteristics of Negro Expression*
Toni Morrison's *Playing in the Dark: Whiteness in the American Literary Imagination*
Edward Said's *Orientalism*
Gayatri Chakravorty Spivak's *Can the Subaltern Speak?*
Mary Wollstonecraft's *A Vindication of the Rights of Women*
Virginia Woolf's *A Room of One's Own*

PHILOSOPHY

Elizabeth Anscombe's *Modern Moral Philosophy*
Hannah Arendt's *The Human Condition*
Aristotle's *Metaphysics*
Aristotle's *Nicomachean Ethics*
Edmund Gettier's *Is Justified True Belief Knowledge?*
Georg Wilhelm Friedrich Hegel's *Phenomenology of Spirit*
David Hume's *Dialogues Concerning Natural Religion*
David Hume's *The Enquiry for Human Understanding*
Immanuel Kant's *Religion within the Boundaries of Mere Reason*
Immanuel Kant's *Critique of Pure Reason*
Søren Kierkegaard's *The Sickness Unto Death*
Søren Kierkegaard's *Fear and Trembling*
C. S. Lewis's *The Abolition of Man*
Alasdair MacIntyre's *After Virtue*
Marcus Aurelius's *Meditations*
Friedrich Nietzsche's *On the Genealogy of Morality*
Friedrich Nietzsche's *Beyond Good and Evil*
Plato's *Republic*
Plato's *Symposium*
Jean-Jacques Rousseau's *The Social Contract*
Gilbert Ryle's *The Concept of Mind*
Baruch Spinoza's *Ethics*
Sun Tzu's *The Art of War*
Ludwig Wittgenstein's *Philosophical Investigations*

POLITICS

Benedict Anderson's *Imagined Communities*
Aristotle's *Politics*
Bernard Bailyn's *The Ideological Origins of the American Revolution*
Edmund Burke's *Reflections on the Revolution in France*
John C. Calhoun's *A Disquisition on Government*
Ha-Joon Chang's *Kicking Away the Ladder*
Hamid Dabashi's *Iran: A People Interrupted*
Hamid Dabashi's *Theology of Discontent: The Ideological Foundation of the Islamic Revolution in Iran*
Robert Dahl's *Democracy and its Critics*
Robert Dahl's *Who Governs?*
David Brion Davis's *The Problem of Slavery in the Age of Revolution*

Alexis De Tocqueville's *Democracy in America*
James Ferguson's *The Anti-Politics Machine*
Frank Dikotter's *Mao's Great Famine*
Sheila Fitzpatrick's *Everyday Stalinism*
Eric Foner's *Reconstruction: America's Unfinished Revolution, 1863-1877*
Milton Friedman's *Capitalism and Freedom*
Francis Fukuyama's *The End of History and the Last Man*
John Lewis Gaddis's *We Now Know: Rethinking Cold War History*
Ernest Gellner's *Nations and Nationalism*
David Graeber's *Debt: the First 5000 Years*
Antonio Gramsci's *The Prison Notebooks*
Alexander Hamilton, John Jay & James Madison's *The Federalist Papers*
Friedrich Hayek's *The Road to Serfdom*
Christopher Hill's *The World Turned Upside Down*
Thomas Hobbes's *Leviathan*
John A. Hobson's *Imperialism: A Study*
Samuel P. Huntington's *The Clash of Civilizations and the Remaking of World Order*
Tony Judt's *Postwar: A History of Europe Since 1945*
David C. Kang's *China Rising: Peace, Power and Order in East Asia*
Paul Kennedy's *The Rise and Fall of Great Powers*
Robert Keohane's *After Hegemony*
Martin Luther King Jr.'s *Why We Can't Wait*
Henry Kissinger's *World Order: Reflections on the Character of Nations and the Course of History*
John Locke's *Two Treatises of Government*
Niccolò Machiavelli's *The Prince*
Thomas Robert Malthus's *An Essay on the Principle of Population*
Mahmood Mamdani's *Citizen and Subject: Contemporary Africa And The Legacy Of Late Colonialism*
Karl Marx's *Capital*
John Stuart Mill's *On Liberty*
John Stuart Mill's *Utilitarianism*
Hans Morgenthau's *Politics Among Nations*
Thomas Paine's *Common Sense*
Thomas Paine's *Rights of Man*
Thomas Piketty's *Capital in the Twenty-First Century*
Robert D. Putnam's *Bowling Alone*
John Rawls's *Theory of Justice*
Jean-Jacques Rousseau's *The Social Contract*
Theda Skocpol's *States and Social Revolutions*
Adam Smith's *The Wealth of Nations*
Sun Tzu's *The Art of War*
Henry David Thoreau's *Civil Disobedience*
Thucydides's *The History of the Peloponnesian War*
Kenneth Waltz's *Theory of International Politics*
Max Weber's *Politics as a Vocation*
Odd Arne Westad's *The Global Cold War: Third World Interventions And The Making Of Our Times*

POSTCOLONIAL STUDIES

Roland Barthes's *Mythologies*
Frantz Fanon's *Black Skin, White Masks*
Homi K. Bhabha's *The Location of Culture*
Gustavo Gutiérrez's *A Theology of Liberation*
Edward Said's *Orientalism*
Gayatri Chakravorty Spivak's *Can the Subaltern Speak?*

The Macat Library By Discipline

PSYCHOLOGY

Gordon Allport's *The Nature of Prejudice*
Alan Baddeley & Graham Hitch's *Aggression: A Social Learning Analysis*
Albert Bandura's *Aggression: A Social Learning Analysis*
Leon Festinger's *A Theory of Cognitive Dissonance*
Sigmund Freud's *The Interpretation of Dreams*
Betty Friedan's *The Feminine Mystique*
Michael R. Gottfredson & Travis Hirschi's *A General Theory of Crime*
Eric Hoffer's *The True Believer: Thoughts on the Nature of Mass Movements*
William James's *Principles of Psychology*
Elizabeth Loftus's *Eyewitness Testimony*
A. H. Maslow's *A Theory of Human Motivation*
Stanley Milgram's *Obedience to Authority*
Steven Pinker's *The Better Angels of Our Nature*
Oliver Sacks's *The Man Who Mistook His Wife For a Hat*
Richard Thaler & Cass Sunstein's *Nudge: Improving Decisions About Health, Wealth and Happiness*
Amos Tversky's *Judgment under Uncertainty: Heuristics and Biases*
Philip Zimbardo's *The Lucifer Effect*

SCIENCE

Rachel Carson's *Silent Spring*
William Cronon's *Nature's Metropolis: Chicago And The Great West*
Alfred W. Crosby's *The Columbian Exchange*
Charles Darwin's *On the Origin of Species*
Richard Dawkin's *The Selfish Gene*
Thomas Kuhn's *The Structure of Scientific Revolutions*
Geoffrey Parker's *Global Crisis: War, Climate Change and Catastrophe in the Seventeenth Century*
Mathis Wackernagel & William Rees's *Our Ecological Footprint*

SOCIOLOGY

Michelle Alexander's *The New Jim Crow: Mass Incarceration in the Age of Colorblindness*
Gordon Allport's *The Nature of Prejudice*
Albert Bandura's *Aggression: A Social Learning Analysis*
Hanna Batatu's *The Old Social Classes And The Revolutionary Movements Of Iraq*
Ha-Joon Chang's *Kicking Away the Ladder*
W. E. B. Du Bois's *The Souls of Black Folk*
Émile Durkheim's *On Suicide*
Frantz Fanon's *Black Skin, White Masks*
Frantz Fanon's *The Wretched of the Earth*
Eric Foner's *Reconstruction: America's Unfinished Revolution, 1863-1877*
Eugene Genovese's *Roll, Jordan, Roll: The World the Slaves Made*
Jack Goldstone's *Revolution and Rebellion in the Early Modern World*
Antonio Gramsci's *The Prison Notebooks*
Richard Herrnstein & Charles A Murray's *The Bell Curve: Intelligence and Class Structure in American Life*
Eric Hoffer's *The True Believer: Thoughts on the Nature of Mass Movements*
Jane Jacobs's *The Death and Life of Great American Cities*
Robert Lucas's *Why Doesn't Capital Flow from Rich to Poor Countries?*
Jay Macleod's *Ain't No Makin' It: Aspirations and Attainment in a Low Income Neighborhood*
Elaine May's *Homeward Bound: American Families in the Cold War Era*
Douglas McGregor's *The Human Side of Enterprise*
C. Wright Mills's *The Sociological Imagination*

Thomas Piketty's *Capital in the Twenty-First Century*
Robert D. Putman's *Bowling Alone*
David Riesman's *The Lonely Crowd: A Study of the Changing American Character*
Edward Said's *Orientalism*
Joan Wallach Scott's *Gender and the Politics of History*
Theda Skocpol's *States and Social Revolutions*
Max Weber's *The Protestant Ethic and the Spirit of Capitalism*

THEOLOGY

Augustine's *Confessions*
Benedict's *Rule of St Benedict*
Gustavo Gutiérrez's *A Theology of Liberation*
Carole Hillenbrand's *The Crusades: Islamic Perspectives*
David Hume's *Dialogues Concerning Natural Religion*
Immanuel Kant's *Religion within the Boundaries of Mere Reason*
Ernst Kantorowicz's *The King's Two Bodies: A Study in Medieval Political Theology*
Søren Kierkegaard's *The Sickness Unto Death*
C. S. Lewis's *The Abolition of Man*
Saba Mahmood's *The Politics of Piety: The Islamic Revival and the Feminist Subject*
Baruch Spinoza's *Ethics*
Keith Thomas's *Religion and the Decline of Magic*

COMING SOON

Chris Argyris's *The Individual and the Organisation*
Seyla Benhabib's *The Rights of Others*
Walter Benjamin's *The Work Of Art in the Age of Mechanical Reproduction*
John Berger's *Ways of Seeing*
Pierre Bourdieu's *Outline of a Theory of Practice*
Mary Douglas's *Purity and Danger*
Roland Dworkin's *Taking Rights Seriously*
James G. March's *Exploration and Exploitation in Organisational Learning*
Ikujiro Nonaka's *A Dynamic Theory of Organizational Knowledge Creation*
Griselda Pollock's *Vision and Difference*
Amartya Sen's *Inequality Re-Examined*
Susan Sontag's *On Photography*
Yasser Tabbaa's *The Transformation of Islamic Art*
Ludwig von Mises's *Theory of Money and Credit*

Macat Disciplines

Access the greatest ideas and thinkers across entire disciplines, including

Postcolonial Studies

Roland Barthes's *Mythologies*
Frantz Fanon's *Black Skin, White Masks*
Homi K. Bhabha's *The Location of Culture*
Gustavo Gutiérrez's *A Theology of Liberation*
Edward Said's *Orientalism*
Gayatri Chakravorty Spivak's *Can the Subaltern Speak?*

Macat analyses are available from all good bookshops and libraries.

Access hundreds of analyses through one, multimedia tool.
Join free for one month **library.macat.com**

Macat Disciplines

Access the greatest ideas and thinkers across entire disciplines, including

AFRICANA STUDIES

Chinua Achebe's *An Image of Africa: Racism in Conrad's Heart of Darkness*

W. E. B. Du Bois's *The Souls of Black Folk*

Zora Neale Hurston's *Characteristics of Negro Expression*

Martin Luther King Jr.'s *Why We Can't Wait*

Toni Morrison's *Playing in the Dark: Whiteness in the American Literary Imagination*

Macat analyses are available from all good bookshops and libraries.

Access hundreds of analyses through one, multimedia tool.
Join free for one month **library.macat.com**

Macat Disciplines

Access the greatest ideas and thinkers across entire disciplines, including

FEMINISM, GENDER AND QUEER STUDIES

Simone De Beauvoir's
The Second Sex

Michel Foucault's
History of Sexuality

Betty Friedan's
The Feminine Mystique

Saba Mahmood's
*The Politics of Piety:
The Islamic Revival and
the Feminist Subject*

Joan Wallach Scott's
*Gender and the
Politics of History*

Mary Wollstonecraft's
*A Vindication of the
Rights of Woman*

Virginia Woolf's
A Room of One's Own

Judith Butler's
Gender Trouble

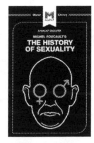

Macat analyses are available from all good bookshops and libraries.

Access hundreds of analyses through one, multimedia tool.
Join free for one month **library.macat.com**

Macat Disciplines

Access the greatest ideas and thinkers across entire disciplines, including

MACAT

CRIMINOLOGY

Michelle Alexander's
The New Jim Crow: Mass Incarceration in the Age of Colorblindness

Michael R. Gottfredson & Travis Hirschi's
A General Theory of Crime

Elizabeth Loftus's
Eyewitness Testimony

Richard Herrnstein & Charles A. Murray's
The Bell Curve: Intelligence and Class Structure in American Life

Jay Macleod's
Ain't No Makin' It: Aspirations and Attainment in a Low-Income Neighborhood

Philip Zimbardo's
The Lucifer Effect

Macat analyses are available from all good bookshops and libraries.

Access hundreds of analyses through one, multimedia tool.
Join free for one month **library.macat.com**

Macat Disciplines

Access the greatest ideas and thinkers across entire disciplines, including

INEQUALITY

Ha-Joon Chang's, *Kicking Away the Ladder*

David Graeber's, *Debt: The First 5000 Years*

Robert E. Lucas's, *Why Doesn't Capital Flow from Rich To Poor Countries?*

Thomas Piketty's, *Capital in the Twenty-First Century*

Amartya Sen's, *Inequality Re-Examined*

Mahbub Ul Haq's, *Reflections on Human Development*

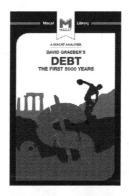

Macat analyses are available from all good bookshops and libraries.

Access hundreds of analyses through one, multimedia tool.
Join free for one month **library.macat.com**

Macat Disciplines

Access the greatest ideas and thinkers across entire disciplines, including

GLOBALIZATION

Arjun Appadurai's, *Modernity at Large: Cultural Dimensions of Globalisation*

James Ferguson's, *The Anti-Politics Machine*

Geert Hofstede's, *Culture's Consequences*

Amartya Sen's, *Development as Freedom*

Macat analyses are available from all good bookshops and libraries.

Access hundreds of analyses through one, multimedia tool.
Join free for one month **library.macat.com**

Macat Disciplines

Access the greatest ideas and thinkers across entire disciplines, including

MAN AND THE ENVIRONMENT

The Brundtland Report's, *Our Common Future*
Rachel Carson's, *Silent Spring*
James Lovelock's, *Gaia: A New Look at Life on Earth*
Mathis Wackernagel & William Rees's, *Our Ecological Footprint*

Macat analyses are available from all good bookshops and libraries.

Access hundreds of analyses through one, multimedia tool.
Join free for one month **library.macat.com**

Macat Disciplines

Access the greatest ideas and thinkers across entire disciplines, including

TOTALITARIANISM

Sheila Fitzpatrick's, *Everyday Stalinism*
Ian Kershaw's, *The "Hitler Myth"*
Timothy Snyder's, *Bloodlands*

Macat Pairs

Analyse historical and modern issues from opposite sides of an argument. Pairs include:

Zora Neale Hurston's
Characteristics of Negro Expression

Using material collected on anthropological expeditions to the South, Zora Neale Hurston explains how expression in African American culture in the early twentieth century departs from the art of white America. At the time, African American art was often criticized for copying white culture. For Hurston, this criticism misunderstood how art works. European tradition views art as something fixed. But Hurston describes a creative process that is alive, ever-changing, and largely improvisational. She maintains that African American art works through a process called 'mimicry'—where an imitated object or verbal pattern, for example, is reshaped and altered until it becomes something new, novel—and worthy of attention.

Frantz Fanon's
Black Skin, White Masks

Black Skin, White Masks offers a radical analysis of the psychological effects of colonization on the colonized.

Fanon witnessed the effects of colonization first hand both in his birthplace, Martinique, and again later in life when he worked as a psychiatrist in another French colony, Algeria. His text is uncompromising in form and argument. He dissects the dehumanizing effects of colonialism, arguing that it destroys the native sense of identity, forcing people to adapt to an alien set of values—including a core belief that they are inferior. This results in deep psychological trauma.

Fanon's work played a pivotal role in the civil rights movements of the 1960s.

Macat analyses are available from all good bookshops and libraries.

Access hundreds of analyses through one, multimedia tool. Join free for one month **library.macat.com**

Macat Pairs

Analyse historical and modern issues from opposite sides of an argument. Pairs include:

INTERNATIONAL RELATIONS IN THE 21ST CENTURY

Samuel P. Huntington's
The Clash of Civilisations

In his highly influential 1996 book, Huntington offers a vision of a post-Cold War world in which conflict takes place not between competing ideologies but between cultures. The worst clash, he argues, will be between the Islamic world and the West: the West's arrogance and belief that its culture is a "gift" to the world will come into conflict with Islam's obstinacy and concern that its culture is under attack from a morally decadent "other."

Clash inspired much debate between different political schools of thought. But its greatest impact came in helping define American foreign policy in the wake of the 2001 terrorist attacks in New York and Washington.

Francis Fukuyama's
The End of History and the Last Man

Published in 1992, *The End of History and the Last Man* argues that capitalist democracy is the final destination for all societies. Fukuyama believed democracy triumphed during the Cold War because it lacks the "fundamental contradictions" inherent in communism and satisfies our yearning for freedom and equality. Democracy therefore marks the endpoint in the evolution of ideology, and so the "end of history." There will still be "events," but no fundamental change in ideology.

Macat Pairs

Analyse historical and modern issues from opposite sides of an argument. Pairs include:

HOW TO RUN AN ECONOMY

John Maynard Keynes's
The General Theory OF Employment, Interest and Money

Classical economics suggests that market economies are self-correcting in times of recession or depression, and tend toward full employment and output. But English economist John Maynard Keynes disagrees.

In his ground-breaking 1936 study *The General Theory*, Keynes argues that traditional economics has misunderstood the causes of unemployment. Employment is not determined by the price of labor; it is directly linked to demand. Keynes believes market economies are by nature unstable, and so require government intervention. Spurred on by the social catastrophe of the Great Depression of the 1930s, he sets out to revolutionize the way the world thinks

Milton Friedman's
The Role of Monetary Policy

Friedman's 1968 paper changed the course of economic theory. In just 17 pages, he demolished existing theory and outlined an effective alternate monetary policy designed to secure 'high employment, stable prices and rapid growth.'

Friedman demonstrated that monetary policy plays a vital role in broader economic stability and argued that economists got their monetary policy wrong in the 1950s and 1960s by misunderstanding the relationship between inflation and unemployment. Previous generations of economists had believed that governments could permanently decrease unemployment by permitting inflation—and vice versa. Friedman's most original contribution was to show that this supposed trade-off is an illusion that only works in the short term.

Macat analyses are available from all good bookshops and libraries.

Access hundreds of analyses through one, multimedia tool.
Join free for one month **library.macat.com**

Macat Pairs

*Analyse historical and modern issues from opposite sides of an argument.
Pairs include:*

Steven Pinker's
The Better Angels of Our Nature

Stephen Pinker's gloriously optimistic 2011 book argues that, despite humanity's biological tendency toward violence, we are, in fact, less violent today than ever before. To prove his case, Pinker lays out pages of detailed statistical evidence. For him, much of the credit for the decline goes to the eighteenth-century Enlightenment movement, whose ideas of liberty, tolerance, and respect for the value of human life filtered down through society and affected how people thought. That psychological change led to behavioral change—and overall we became more peaceful. Critics countered that humanity could never overcome the biological urge toward violence; others argued that Pinker's statistics were flawed.

Philip Zimbardo's
The Lucifer Effect

Some psychologists believe those who commit cruelty are innately evil. Zimbardo disagrees. In *The Lucifer Effect*, he argues that sometimes good people do evil things simply because of the situations they find themselves in, citing many historical examples to illustrate his point. Zimbardo details his 1971 Stanford prison experiment, where ordinary volunteers playing guards in a mock prison rapidly became abusive. But he also describes the tortures committed by US army personnel in Iraq's Abu Ghraib prison in 2003—and how he himself testified in defence of one of those guards. committed by US army personnel in Iraq's Abu Ghraib prison in 2003—and how he himself testified in defence of one of those guards.

Macat Pairs

Analyse historical and modern issues from opposite sides of an argument. Pairs include:

HOW WE RELATE TO EACH OTHER AND SOCIETY

Jean-Jacques Rousseau's
The Social Contract

Rousseau's famous work sets out the radical concept of the 'social contract': a give-and-take relationship between individual freedom and social order.

If people are free to do as they like, governed only by their own sense of justice, they are also vulnerable to chaos and violence. To avoid this, Rousseau proposes, they should agree to give up some freedom to benefit from the protection of social and political organization. But this deal is only just if societies are led by the collective needs and desires of the people, and able to control the private interests of individuals. For Rousseau, the only legitimate form of government is rule by the people.

Robert D. Putnam's
Bowling Alone

In *Bowling Alone*, Robert Putnam argues that Americans have become disconnected from one another and from the institutions of their common life, and investigates the consequences of this change.

Looking at a range of indicators, from membership in formal organizations to the number of invitations being extended to informal dinner parties, Putnam demonstrates that Americans are interacting less and creating less "social capital" – with potentially disastrous implications for their society.

It would be difficult to overstate the impact of *Bowling Alone*, one of the most frequently cited social science publications of the last half-century.

Printed in the United States
by Baker & Taylor Publisher Services